THE
ABIDE
GUIDE

LIVING LIKE LEBOWSKI

Oliver Benjamin & Dwayne Eutsey

Ulysses Press

Published by:
Ulysses Press
P.O. Box 3440
Berkeley, CA 94703
www.ulyssespress.com

ISBN: 978-1-56975-976-9
Library of Congress Control Number: 2011926014

Printed in the United States by Bang Printing

10 9 8 7 6 5 4 3 2 1

Acquisitions Editor: Kelly Reed
Managing Editor: Claire Chun
Editor: Barbara Schultz
Proofreader: Elyce Petker
Production: Judith Metzener
Interior illustrations: © Brandon Yarwood except on page 244
    © Andrea Miranda Atenas
Front cover illustration: © Brandon Yarwood

Distributed by Publishers Group West

THE
ABIDE
GUIDE

To all the Dudeist priests around the world.
Proud we are of all of you.
Lord, you can imagine where it goes from here.

CONTENTS

I. Innerductions 9

In the Beginning Was the Dude Way 10

The Whole Durn Dudeist Comedy 14

The Dude Testament 22

II. Wiser Fellers Than Ourselves—Dudeist History 75

Great Dudes in History 76

The Book of Revolutions: Dudeist Prophecy 107

Dudeist Movements: Dudeism Down
    Through the Ages 117

Creating a More Dude-ocratic Society: The Politics
    of the Dude 129

Cinema Verte: Stoner Films and *The Big Lebowski* 143

Subjects Like Women: Dudeist Feminism 156

III. *Making It to Practice—Dudeist Lifestyle and Techniques* 176

Self-Help Chopperin' In: The Dudeism Helping
  to Abide Movement (DHAM) 177

Duderinos Unanimous: A 12-Step Program
  for Personal Dudevolution 192

Dudeitation: Just Drop in to See What
  Condition Your Condition Is In 199

This Aggression Will Not Stand: Dude-Jitsu,
  the Dudeist Art of Self-Defense 206

Some Kind of Yoga: A Natural, Zesty Exercise 218

Thankie: The Power of Dudeiversal Energy 234

Fungin' Shway: The Dudeist Science of
  Really Tying Your Room Together 242

Dude Economics 250

Epilogue: I Can Get You a Vow 253

About the Authors 256

I

Innerductions

IN THE BEGINNING WAS THE DUDE WAY...

I wouldn't call the Dude Way a Deity, 'cause what's a *Deity*?

The Dude Way, well, it fits right in there as the lazy source of this here universe. Verily, though, it did not run around trying to create this time and place in a single week. That would have been too exhausting, even with the seventh day off.

No, across the spans of time, the Dude Way just took it easy, warshing along the ever-expanding cusp of the cosmos like fresh cream pouring into a bottomless sea of dark Kahlúa. And wherever the Dude Way abided, there emerged naturally an infinite array of suns, and planets, and galaxies, and other universes, and what-have-you.

And that was cool. That was cool.

Over countless eons, the Dude Way unfolded an intricate web of life throughout the vast universe. Everything in that web was interconnected to everything else in the web and everything grooved together in cosmic balance through the Dude Way.

And that was cool. That was cool.

A small part of that cosmic web of life consisted of some forms of life I want to tell you about, some life-forms by the name of human beings. Now, these human beings grew from a pale blue dot somewhere in the remote regions of the cosmos—and this dot was called Earth. For a time, these life-forms abided in harmony with the natural rhythms of the Dude Way.

Just walking around, throwing rocks, having the occasional mushroom flashback.

And that was cool. That was cool.

But then many human beings forgot the Dude Way and their thinking about the purpose of life became too uptight. They made up things called weekdays, and jobs, and infomercials and ran around much of their lives wondering where to find something else they made up called *the money*.

Instead of humans who were simply being, they had become overachieving humans. And verily, it was sore exhausting.

Throughout millennia of negative energy, some humans looked around and saw all the stress talking and said, "Fuck it." And they abided in the Dude Way, just taking it easy for all us uptight sinners out here.

And that was cool. That was cool.

Every so often, these Great Dudes would ramble around reminding the overachieving humans about takin' 'er easy in the Dude Way. Many humans wondered what in God's holy name these Great Dudes were blathering about. Some of the exhausted humans, though, were listening to the Great Dudes' story. And they did yearn to turn away from a world gone crazy and simply abide.

And lo, on March 6, 1998, they became like little children who wandered into the middle of a movie when the Coen Brothers' *The Big Lebowski* appeared in a multiplex near you. And the glory of the Dude Way (embodied by the Dude) was projected onto the collective consciousness around the pale blue dot. And, with the exception of some reactionary movie critics, many humans were verily amused and wanted to turn away from overachieving and return to simply being.

And the movie said unto them, "The Dude abides…Take comfort in that."

And this became a sign unto humans everywhere: "Ye shall abide, too, even in the middle of a weekday, dressed like that."

And suddenly there was with the movie a great multi-dude abiding in the Dude Way, many of them bowling, drinking Caucasians, listening to whale songs, wearing bathrobes to supermarkets, going out to look for a cash machine, having occasional acid flashbacks, and proclaiming to the pale blue dot: "Is this a...what day is this?"

And that was cool. Fabulous stuff, man.

THE WHOLE DURN DUDEIST COMEDY

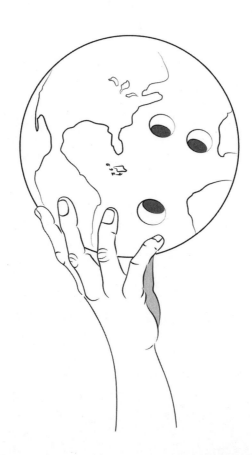

Pre-Ramble

We, the Dudeists, in order to form a more perfect groovin', establish just taking it easy, and promote inner tranquility, do ordain and establish this guide on abiding.

For in this world there are two paths you can go by, as a Great Dude in history once crooned.

There's the uptight way and there's the Dude Way.

Rushing down the uptight way, chasing after bullshit money that never existed anyway, you race past important things in life like enjoying some burgers, some beers, and a few laughs, only to crash too soon into the end of your life, where you're left wondering, "Aw, man, what's that smell?"

It's a bummer, man.

Fortunately, there's an exit you can take from the uptight way. It's a route we want to tell you about...something called abiding in the Dude Way, an ancient, almost-forgotten road that sidesteps the seamy valleys, ransom hand-offs, and abutment lodgings of life.

That's what this here book aims to do. But before we get started, we'd like to answer a question that some of our readers are probably asking right about now.

What the Fuck Are We Blathering About?

That's a fair enough question.

Although there are over 120,000 ordained Dudeist priests around the world currently taking it easy for all you sinners out there, that still leaves 5,999,880,000 people (give or take a few) who have absolutely no clue what the Church of the Latter-Dude is or what Dudeism is all about.[1]

As founders of the world's slowest-growing religion, we're cool with that. All that proselytizing and converting, condemning and persecuting, crusading and jihading that some of our compeers in the world's Big Beliefskis go through to feed the bull-dogma...well, it all just seems exhausting.

It's certainly not the kind of missionary position we prefer.

Still, with so many folks living such stressed-out lives these days, we've decided to put aside our strict regimen of lounging around on our holy hammocks and sacred sofas to enlighten up an uptight world that's apparently gone crazy.

Why? Because we believe that times like these call for living more like Lebowski...and we're talking about the Dude here.

The Dudeist Frame of Reference

For Dudeists, *The Big Lebowski* is more than just a movie. It's a way of life, the philosophical rug that really ties the universe together.

That's a hefty claim to make about a film, especially one that flopped when the Coen Brothers released it back in 1998. It may even sound downright silly or even sacrilegious for us to make such a claim about something that is, after all, merely entertainment.

---

1 If you want more information, would like to be ordained (it's free and easy, just like our ethos), or want to chat with other Dudely types, visit dudeism.com. It's your answer for everything.

However, we're not trying to scam anyone here. If we understand it correctly, "mere" entertainment has always been an essential part of religious life, especially in Western civilization. Ancient Greek comedies and tragedies, for example, were integral to Athens' sacred civic ceremonies. Medieval morality plays promoted Christian values to a wide audience more effectively than priests blathering Latin from the pulpit. These forms of mere entertainment served the vital function of unifying folks into communities and helped to create, promote, and reinforce the very ethos of our culture.

We agree with many wiser fellers than ourselves who say that movies serve a similar purpose today. Filmmakers reach into the same deep, mythic pools that their theatrical forebears plumbed to create narratives they hope will resonate profoundly with viewers. George Lucas did for *Star Wars*, Francis Ford Coppola did for *Apocalypse Now*, and Adam Sandler did for...well, not all films are life-changing.

Still, even in films dismissed as escapist diversions, what draws viewers to them at some level is an enduring mythic (and often unconscious) hope that through the light projected on the movie screen they'll see themselves up close, as the band U2 once put it. The stories we create, after all, whether told around a campfire, written in a book, performed on a stage, or projected onto a screen, usually end up creating us as well.

That's why we believe *The Big Lebowski* is more than just a "cult film." Cults, after all, are on the fringe. Yet with its millions of fans (according to Facebook), *The Big Lebowski* might better be described as "religious." Anyway, that's the way the worldwide Dudeist movement sees it. What is a religion, after all, but a cult that caught on?

It's not just about popularity, of course, otherwise, *Titanic* would have its own religion too. In religious texts and figureheads and characters we discover our deeper selves. And though the movie's main character is a slacker who calls himself the Dude, his eyes are a blue million miles.[2] In other words, he fits right in there in our collective unconscious-ness, comforting all of us uptight, downsized, single-minded, multitasking, overworked, underpaid, plugged-in, pissed-off, shit-on, run-down, zoned-out sinners by embodying what life is truly all about.

We're talking about *taking it easy, man.*

Yes, it's really that simple. Unfortunately, though, it's a message the square community doesn't give a shit about. Keeping us uptight, after all, helps them keep the baksheesh. Though the Dude was dismissed as a bum by overachievers like the millionaire Mr. Lebowski, and as a deadbeat by real reactionaries like the Sherriff of Malibu, we recognize him as a bona fide hee-ro. That is, the modern epitome of a long, lazy tradition of Dudes (both fictional and historical) re-vered across the sands of time for reminding us, in different ways and in different places around the world, to just chill the fuck out.

The problem is, most of these revered Dudes who once personified and vivified the Dude Way in their time and place are today no longer openly associated with the Dude word.

---

2 This is a line taken from the Captain Beefheart song on the soundtrack. Though the Dude's eyes are in fact a piercing blue, there's not a literal connection.

Pan, the lazy Greek god, for instance, may have been pretty well regarded back in his day, but he no longer draws much water in our pious, preachy communities.[3] And languid philosophies like early Christianity and Buddhism have become oddly achievement-oriented since their uncompromised first drafts. It seems that where Great Dudes were once an integral part of the whole durn human comedy, they've gradually been swept under the rug, so to speak.

That's why we founded the Church of the Latter-Day Dude: to bring this Dude shit back to light, man. As we explain on our website:

> While Dudeism in its official form has been organized as a religion only recently, it has existed down through the ages in one form or another. Probably the earliest form of Dudeism was the original form of Chinese Taoism, before it went all weird with magic tricks and body fluids. The originator of Taoism, Lao Tzu, basically said "smoke 'em if you got 'em," and "mellow out, man," although he said this in ancient Chinese so something may have been lost in the translation.
>
> Down through the ages, this "rebel shrug" has fortified many successful creeds: Buddhism, Christianity, Sufism, John Lennonism, and Fo'-Shizzle-my-Nizzlism. The idea is this: Life is short and complicated, and nobody knows what to

---

3 That's partly because the real reactionaries pinned the whole loss-of-paradise thing on him by drawing the devil in his image. They figured, here's a loser, a deadbeat, someone the square community won't give a shit about.

do about it. So don't do anything about it. Just take it easy, man. Stop worrying so much whether you'll make it into the finals. Kick back with some friends and some oat soda, and whether you roll strikes or gutters, do your best to be true to yourself and others—that is to say, abide.[4]

This here *Abide Guide* is meant to help you do just that.

The Abide Guide

Starting things off, the first chapter provides an overall frame of reference so we're not like a child wandering into the middle of a movie. "The Dude Testament" takes in the "big picture." In doing so, it ferrets out the life lessons contained in our Sacred Source (*The Big Lebowski*) and explains how you can apply them to your life.

The rest of the book is organized around two broad areas that explore this central theme:

- **"Wiser Fellers than Ourselves—Dudeist History,"** in which we place our ethos within time's larger frame of reference, spanning from prehistoric nomads getting stoned around pot-fueled bonfires to Dudeist feminism. Learning our Dudeist heritage is important because those who forget the past are doomed to... um...aw, hell, lost my train of thought there.
- **"Making It to Practice—Dudeist Lifestyle and Techniques,"** where we explore the eternal adage, "I Dude, therefore, I am." And we provide various practical ways

---

4 dudeism.com/whatisdudeism

to help you abide in a hectic world, such as Dudeist spiritual and self-help techniques, our 12-step program for personal Dudevolution, and the ancient martial art of Dude-jitsu.

And, welp, that about does 'er. Wraps 'er all up. Parts, anyway.

In addition to making you laugh to beat the band, we hope this guide will be something like a GPS that helps you discern the Dude Way in your own life, only without that annoying prerecorded voice always telling you where to turn. Because we're not a bunch of fascists here, man. We can't tell you specifically where to find the Dude Way. With that in mind, maybe this book is more like a "GFS," a literary device that reminds you to "Go with the Flow, Slowly."

Because once we're on that path, dudes, we've already reached our Dudestination. And we can take comfort in that. Be there, man.

THE DUDE TESTAMENT

All I Need to Know
I Learned from Watching
The Big Lebowski

The big picture! It's hard to see sometimes. Whether we're looking at it from a little bungalow on Venice Beach or a huge mansion in Pasadena, our thinking about life can become very uptight. There are so many strands to keep in our heads, man. It can be stupefyin'. What we need is something to help tie it all together. Luckily there are ways, dude. I can get you a TOE (theory of everything) by three o'clock. Or maybe you're just looking for a well-woven tapestry of ideas, a foundation that will make you feel at home in the world. If that's what you're after, then listen to this a-here *Big Lebowski* analysis we're about to unfold. It'll really help you make sense of the whole durn human comedy. Parts, anyway. We're talking about *Dudeism* here.

There have already been lots of those so-called "theories of everything," which purport to sum up what life's all about. For most of human history, TOEs have been conveyed through tall tales and scribbles on walls, and later through books and organized religion and law. But today people are busy, as I know you are. So the most popular way to step back and take in the "big picture" is through the compressed frame of reference that cinema provides. Now, many learned men have disputed this, but we believe that *The Big Lebowski* is the film for our time and place, high in the running for best movie ever, and so it makes a purty good substitute for all those severed TOEs scattered about out there.[5]

Okay then, what makes *The Big Lebowski* the most important—nay, most *religious*—movie of our day and age? It's an important question. Like most great books or philosophies or religions, the most powerful moving pictures help us perceive a much broader portion of the world than we normally witness in the course of our day-to-day lives. And, what's more, they do so without straying too far from the center of humanity. In the parlance of *The Big Lebowski*, they really tie our ruminations together.

For a brief two hours, great movies provide us with certain information. New shit comes to light and we are made privy to it. How much we dig the story that unfolds before us is usually determined by how broadly and deeply that light penetrates us. In other words, truly great movies shine light upon the whole durn human comedy. Not just the parts.

In the Coens' case, a lot has to do with their use of the wide-angle lens. Filmmakers who employ wide angles draw the viewer more intimately into the frame of reference. And the Coen Brothers are the uncontested philosopher kings of

---

5 TOE is in fact a common abbreviation for "Theory of Everything," at least among physicists. Where religions once provided "theories of everything," the current scientific search for this has to do with a mathematical model that would incorporate all the fragmented theories of physics into one elegant whole. Interestingly, one of the fellows leading the charge is Garrett Lisi, a surfer Dude based in Maui who lives in his van (sometimes). When we contacted him about this he replied, "I can get you a TOE by three o'clock!" Far out. Dudeism has compeers in high places. See: http://bit.ly/10nCT.

wide angles.[6] I'm not just talking about interactive hardware here—not only do they employ the widest angle lenses in their films of any auteurs in Hollywood, they also examine a broader view of the human condition than just about anyone in the league. And though it might not seem so at first, *The Big Lebowski* is likely their widest. And wildest. It's a purty good story too—makes us feel all warm inside.

Moreover, though it may not be evident upon first viewing (or second, or even the tenth), *The Big Lebowski* might well be the "widest" film in history. It stands (or slouches) alongside other great works of literature that tried to tie all of humanity together: Dante's *Inferno*. Melville's *Moby Dick*. Homer's *Odyssey*. The Bible. Compeers, you know?

Surely one of the reasons people find such inspiration and solace in *The Big Lebowski* is that, like those other far-seeing works of literature, it sits on a bluff overlooking valleys and oceans, peering over the past and future horizons of civilization. With humor and humanity, it teaches mankind how to "fit right in there." Consequently, like other great pieces of literature that are still argued over and discussed and quoted long after they were composed, *The Big Lebowski* seems destined for the same sort of immortality. No other film has engendered so much scholarly speculation in such a short time, and no other film has engendered such ardent fans with such a propensity to employ its parlance in common conversation. And though some dismiss it as a ludicrous stoner comedy with a ridiculous plot (see "*Cinema Verte*,"

---

6 Chapter 6 in Robertson and Cooke's *The Big Lebowski: The Making of a Coen Brothers Film* delves widely into this.

page 143), no other film provides such a welcome frame of reference for our time and place. We take comfort in that.

What follows is our attempt to ferret out the essential lessons of the film and how to incorporate them into the "big picture" of your own life. We'll mosey along the trail of the film with you, pointing out important lookouts along the way from the back of our high horse. You may not agree with everything we have to say, but remember, this is all just, like, our opinion, man. Take from this what you dig and forget about any TOEs we might accidentally step on or cut off. We're not trying to scam anyone here. No harm intended. More than anything else, we're sympathizing here, dude.

The Lebowski Liturgy: Lessons for Living Like Lebowski

1. You can die with a smile on your face without feeling like the good Lord gypped you.

As if paying homage to the earliest human art form, the story starts off with a simple campfire chat, just as cavemen did around the burning branches eons ago. An elderly cowboy narrator starts us off by unfolding a tall tale about a tumbling tumbleweed—namely, an unemployed former hippie in the early 1990s, around the time of "our conflict with Sad'm and the Eye-rackies." The narrator seems wildly out of place to comment on something happening in such a contemporary setting, but keep in mind that *The Big Lebowski* is shot in such a wide angle that it could be said to transcend the laws of space and time.

What is it that is so special about the shlumpy main character that can inspire such awe and admiration in our narrator? Certainly it's not his wardrobe (flip-flops and a bathrobe), nor his wealth (he has to pay for a carton of half-and-half with a postdated check[7]), nor his nickname ("Dude—that's a name no one would self-apply where I come from"). Nevertheless, the Stranger assures us that the Dude is "the man for his time and place." In fact, the cowboy is so dumbstruck by the Dude that he loses his train of thought halfway through the introduction. We're pretty baffled ourselves.

And just what is that time and place exactly? That's the end of the 20th century, in Los Angeles, the city of angels. It's the limit of the great 3,000-year westward expansion, and the end of a particular era marked by unprecedented violence and ideological extremism. Most of those ideologies turned out just plain wrong, even though millions of people died face down in the muck fighting in their defense. Now, with nowhere left to go, his horse hitched to a post alongside the bosom of the Pacific Ocean, the cowboy is obliged to make sense of it all. What's it all about? It's a question that people have asked for ages, sure, but perhaps is more salient today than ever. So much is happening so fast that "it all" has become a swiftly moving target. Luckily, the Stranger's encounter with the Dude and his story provides an answer he

---

7 The date on the check he's writing as he watches George Bush initiate a war of Biblical proportions upon Iraq? September 11, 1991. Ten years to the day before the consequences of that "aggression" would be made clear. This really freaks people out. But we assure you, it's not a prophecy. The Dude is just a man, man.

finds acceptable, one that can put a smile on his face before darkness finally warshes over. Hopefully it will do so for us as well.

2. Allow there are some nice folks out there.

First of all, the narrator is a friendly guy. That's evident right off the bat. "They call Los Ang-elees the City of Angels. I didn't find it to be that exactly, but I will allow there are some nice folks there."[8]

The fact that he's essentially kindly is one of the reasons he's the only feller in the film who truly sees the Dude for what he is: an unlikely savior, despite his outward appearance and strange moniker. If you're not going to approach "the whole durn human comedy" with an open, affable attitude, then you're not going to get the point. Friendliness is the only asset you can share that doesn't cost you anything— and in fact makes you richer the more you give it away. It's the ultimate anti-gyp,[9] a pyramid scheme inverted.

In a day and age marked by greed, mistrust, and corruption, where neighbors don't even know each other and people are divided along party lines, religious lines, lifestyle lines, and all variety of other arbitrary squiggles in the sand, it's

---

8 The city's name comes from "Nuestra Senora la Reina de los Angeles" (Our Lady the Queen of the Angels)—that is, the Catholic Virgin Mary. No actual angels were ever thought to have spent any time in Los Angeles.

9 Though the Stranger says, "I can die with a smile on my face without feelin' like the good Lord gypped me," he's using a term many consider offensive, an epithet for gypsies, who were seen to be dishonest in commerce. But the Dude's philosophy can be said to honor that of the gypsies. Parts, anyway. Is the Dude a gypsy king?

easy to forget just how much we have in common. It seems as if we have been divided and conquered by the interests of others, not our own. Yet our differences are far more minor than we are led to believe. And though the Stranger is so friendly and accommodating that it borders on the humorously anachronistic, it is the Dude who truly raises humanistic fellow-feeling to the level that Socrates, the Buddha, and Jesus intended. *Shoosh*. Three thousand years of civilization really lost its train of thought there. (See "Dudeist Movements," page 117.)

3. It's down there somewhere, let me take another look.

The story starts in earnest with the Dude arriving home to his modest Venice bungalow with his carton of half-and-half, only to be assaulted by thugs who have broken into his house. "Where's the money, Lebowski?" one shouts while shoving the Dude's head in his toilet. Even during this distressing interlude, the Dude is accommodating and clever enough to joke, "It's down there somewhere, let me take another look."

When *The Big Lebowski* came out in 1998, it too went straight into the toilet. *Where was the money, Lebowski?* It barely made back its investment. Luckily, it was indeed down there somewhere, and people did eventually take another look. In retrospect we now know that its original failure was because it was too unprecedented, too complex, and just too plain weird for audiences to digest right away. Even die-hard fans contend it takes at least three viewings before the whole thing begins to make sense, to snap into focus. And yet, life is far more complicated and unpredictable than a standard

Hollywood movie—more like *The Big Lebowski*, actually. The plot doesn't make sense, for one thing. Maybe the problem with life is the same as the problem with *Lebowski*: We just don't give it enough chances to explain itself to us. And we expect it to make sense and wrap up all the loose ends. Fat chance! Life is an endless string of funny *shtuff*, language problems, and ringers being thrown out for ringers.

Even the Dude admits, later in the film, that his thinking "has been very uptight" and that certain assumptions had prevented him from solving the movie's central mystery. We who have taken *The Big Lebowski* as a commentary on what life is all about make it a point to be on guard against our own "uptight thinking." We have to try to treat the world in the same way as we treat the movie—as a complicated case, but one that we can enjoy nonetheless, if we keep our minds flexible enough. In the end it may not be a problem to solve, but a story to enjoy.

4. Don't say "hero," 'cause what's a hero?

There once was a time in cinema where the good guys wore white and the bad guys wore black, and their moral behavior was just as Old Testament as their hats. But of course, that got old fast. These days our grey matter is far more interested in the grey areas. In response to this didactic haberdashery, movies soon enjoyed the rise of the "antihero"—that is, someone who may not be 100 percent morally upstanding, but whom we nevertheless sympathize with, because we ourselves are morally closer to Silver than to the Lone Ranger.

In the mid-20th century, perhaps as a response to three major wars and the horror they produced, along with the dark side of a growing urbanization, the dystopian *film noir* genre took hold. *Film noir* was characterized by a strong male lead who was somewhat of an antisocial creep, yet who proved to be morally head and shoulders above those around him. Nowadays, these so-called antiheroes are everywhere in Hollywood. They've Bogarted the joint, in the parlance of our times.

Yet, these characters are antiheroes in affect only. Though *noir* heroes' clothing may tend to be black in color, they're still purveying a strict interpretation of white-hat cowboy morality—namely, it is the hero's job to go out into the world and do his best to "do the right thing, no matter what the cost."

Conversely, the Dude (whose clothing tellingly tends toward earth tones) may be the only real antihero in the history of film. Why? Because he is so utterly, unapologetically unheroic. Whereas most heroes are marked by complacency at the beginning, they are ultimately called into action by a stark necessity. The Dude is the exact opposite: Though we learn that he was an activist for civil liberties in his youth, he has done virtually nothing in the intervening decades. "My career's slowed down a little lately," he notes, without a trace of wistfulness. Whenever the "call to action" came in his life, the Dude let his answering machine take a message. *The Big Lebowski* chronicles perhaps the only thing he has actually "done" since his student days. Only, it's not even his choice. Others basically Shanghai him into action.

Perhaps we're meant to laugh at him at first; but given what we are forced to consider later in the film regarding the so-called heroism of military and business titans, it appears that the Dude's laid-back, utterly *passive-ist* approach to life may, in fact, be a perfectly heroic crusade. Part of the problem is that activism is such hard work. But Dudeism, on the other hand, is a crusade that the average person can easily incorporate into his or her life. And while some might find this a selfish lifestyle, what social scientists now know about the nature of happiness suggests the opposite. Merely acting as an example of self-contentment and non-aggression has a powerfully calming influence on everyone we come in contact with.[10] In other words, Dudeness is a highly contagious form of communicable *ease*. Notice how much affection the Dude generates from all those around him—he even brings a measure of comfort to human "paraquat" and known pornographers.

5. There's a little you should ask.

Let's not beat around the Bush. The film starts with Bush the Elder declaring war on Iraq. Now, in spite of all the philosophical and ideological pronouncements, if there's one thing Desert Storm was really all about, it was the "fucking money." Yet there's nothing strange about this. Money is one of the principal pillars of civilization. Are you surprised at our tiers? Gotta feed the monolith.[11]

---

10 *Dudespaper* article concerning this research: http://bit.ly/elm1sy.

11 This is underscored at the end of the film by Walter Sobchak's own determination that the Gulf War was "all about oil." It is possible that this was the first commercial film to outwardly espouse this idea. *Three Kings*

In *The Big Lebowski*, characters may espouse the value of work, heroism, freedom, story, production value, feelings, and so on, but what they're all really after is more money and power. "Where's the money, Lebowski?" is the refrain underlying the entire wild 118-minute ride, even as it's camouflaged by all varieties of competing philosophies, lifestyles, and ethical proclamations. Well, all except for those of the Dude, of course. All he expressly wants is to get his rug back (the thugs pissed on it before they left). However, even this modest fragment of material want ends up affording him all sorts of woe.[12]

The Dude thus provides an example of exalted ordinariness and humility, which we might all aspire to if we ever want to enjoy this a-here story you're about to unfold. Looked at through the long (and wide!) lens of history, everyone is astonishingly ordinary. The words of proto-Dude Oscar Wilde seem especially apt in a bowling alley decorated extensively with "googie" motifs: *We are all of us in the gutter, but some of us are looking at the stars.*[13]

As if to set the stage for this Dudeist ideal, the opening credit sequence may be one of the most beautiful bal-

---

and the famous scene with Mark Wahlberg being forced to drink oil came out a year later. Perhaps that's why Walter's assertion is muffled by the sounds of bowling: People weren't ready to accept this idea yet.

12 "Wasn't it Jack Kerouac who said, 'If you own a rug, you own too much?'" Ed Burns, *Confidence* (2003).

13 " We are all of us in the gutter, but some of us are looking at the stars." Oscar Wilde, *Lady Windermere's Fan*, 1892. Wilde may have introduced the term "dude" to U.S. shores. See "Dude Defined": http://bit.ly/bJnIqe. "Googie" stars were an important part of 1950s space-age design—the era of suburban bowling alleys and lofty post-war aspirations.

lets of ordinariness ever filmed. A standing army of extras bowl in slow motion, showcasing a wide variety of everyday folks having a grand old time. It's easy to forget, with all the beauty and makeup and stylishness inherent in cinematic production, that we are in fact these roly-poly rollers, not dramatic heroes or villains. And thank Dude for *that*. That sounds exhausting.

6. You're like a child who wanders into the middle of a movie.

It turns out the thugs mistook the Dude for another Jeffrey Lebowski, a millionaire, whose wife owed money to their boss, a porn mogul named Jackie Treehorn. The next day, the Dude tells the story of the rug to his belligerent Vietnam vet best friend, Walter, who suggests he try to get compensation from the guy whose rug was meant to be pissed on in the first place. You know, just like in the Bible. Rugcompense. A wee for a wee.[14]

As they're arguing about this, their bowling teammate Donny keeps asking what they're talking about. Walter scolds him that he's out of his element. "You're like a child who wanders into the middle of a movie!" he says, refusing to fill him in. There is no reason why Walter should be so impatient, other than the fact that he's desperate to fix immediately what he considers to be a matter of critical importance. In

---

14 An eye for an eye came originally from the Babylonian (present day Iraq) "Code of Hammurabi" before it was adopted into the ancient Jewish canon. This "code" contains some of the most horrific punishments ever dreamed up by humankind. So, though "an eye for an eye" morality may still be popular, taking it in context might reveal its correlative brutality.

other words, he is an action hero in the classic sense of the word. No time to argue. Chop chop!

Only problem is, it's not a matter of critical importance. It's only pee stains on a rug.

We are all like children who wander into the middle of a movie—every moment of our lives. Our lives are stories of unending complexity. Far too often, the best thing to do is to just say, "Fuck it, let's go bowling" instead of drawing a line in the sand and laying down the law. Had Walter and the Dude just acknowledged this from the start, none of the troubles that follow would have happened. If there's one thing we learned in *The Big Lebowski*...when the world kicks you, don't kick back. In most cases, it's a better idea to *kick-back* and try to enjoy the cycle.

7. Take the road less rambled.

The Dude takes Walter's advice and visits the millionaire Lebowski. Before the meeting, the millionaire's toady assistant Brandt takes the Dude on a tour of Mr. Lebowski's "various commendations" hanging on the wall of his office, all of them expressly mentioning the word "achievement" in one way or another. This is obviously in stark contrast to our non-hero Jeffrey Lebowski's life of non-achievement. However, instead of feeling blue about it, it's clear that the Dude couldn't care less. Despite this rare opportunity to see what vast riches and honors he might have accrued had he applied himself in college instead of smoking "Thai stick" and "occupying various administration buildings," the Dude seems pretty content with his choices. Robert Frost's poem "The Road Not Taken" suggests that life is full of forks in the road and that we have to be happy with the choices we've made. It is an attitude of nearly Nietzschean integrity, one that few of us are *düdermensch* enough to actually pull off.[15]

8. Nihilism is exhausting.

Of course, the Big Lebowski angrily refuses to reimburse the Dude for the soiled rug, calling him a "bum."[16] But rather than waste his energy fighting about it, the Dude says, "Fuck it," and leaves. Despite the tongue–lashing, he's in a good mood. He takes a rug from the house anyway and proceeds to flirt with a sexy young woman in a bikini sunbathing by the swimming pool.

But this, in fact, turns out to be Bunny, Lebowski's wife, the one who started all the trouble in the first place by owing money to Jackie Treehorn! Not only is she salaciously flirty with the Dude, but she also nonchalantly points out her

---

15 German philosopher Friedrich Nietzsche imagined the coming of a new type of man, an *übermensch* (overman or superman), who would free himself from the bonds of religious and cultural conditioning and truly think freely. He also addressed the idea of "eternal recurrence" in which all events will occur over and over again in our universe, the acceptance of which should inspire not horror, but a form of contentment, at least in "great" men. Though both the fascists (like the other Lebowski) and the nihilists (like Uli) championed the ideas of Nietzsche, most scholars contend that neither actually understood his ideas properly. We think Nietzsche would have been pretty impressed with the Dude, though— he is both a truly free thinker, and at the same time appears wholly content with all the events in his life, unsavory as some of them may seem to others.

16 It is important to mention that "bum" comes from the German *bummler*, meaning "loafer," and originally had nothing to do with the idea of mooching. A bum was a lazy person, but not necessarily a drain on society.

boyfriend, passed out drunk in the pool. He's a nihilist, she explains: "He doesn't care about anything." "Oh, that must be exhausting," the Dude replies, joking about his unconscious state. But there's more to it than that—though the Dude stands in stark contrast to the big over-arching *ideoloskies* of the 20th century, he also stands apart from their annihilating opposite, nihilism: the belief that nothing means anything.

After 20th-century science finally shot out the tires of religion, and then two world wars slid down the shorts of science, the notion that life was utterly pointless took hold among some of the more sensitive members of Western society. Nevertheless, the notion that "nothing means anything" runs so counter to everyday human experience that only German philosophers, mystical gurus, and teenage Goths have ever been able to convincingly pull it off.

Unlike those who, like the ubercapitalist Lebowski, adhere to static philosophies etched in stone, or their counterparts—like Uli Kunkel—who embrace a nihilistic postmodernism that threatens to liquidate all structure and human accomplishment, the Dude merely says, "Fuck it," and excuses himself from the argument. To the Dudeist way of thinking, life is a liquid being passed from temporary container to temporary container. It's a distinctly pragmatic approach to making sense of this strange movie that we've all walked into the middle of. What's your drink, Dude? Naturally, it's mostly half-and-half.

9. Will you just take it easy, man?

So far, the movie has served up two examples of what the Dude is not: He is neither an ideologue, nor a nihilist. Now we get to see yet another prime example of the *un-Dude*—his best buddy, Walter Sobchak. They say opposites attract—this universal principle is apparently at the base of this unlikely friendship.

Walter's weakness is not vanity (like the other Lebowski), nor is it vacancy (like Uli)—rather, it is violence. Back in the bowling alley, Walter stands up for everything he holds sacred by pointing his handgun at an opponent who disagrees with Walter's assertion that his toe has slipped over the line during a turn. It is such an outrageous response to such a minor infraction that we howl with laughter. Yet overreactions like this occur every day and they invoke howls of a different sort. And often we're the ones waving around the figurative firearms. Uncontrolled anger makes S.O.B.s out of all of us.

As they leave the alley, just ahead of the police, the Dude begs Walter to "just take it easy, man!" It is a refrain that will repeat at various times throughout the film—one of the most defining phrases of the Dude. Though a hackneyed old hippie bon mot, it's more applicable today than ever. A few decades of "can-do" ambition and eagerness have obscured the fact that the entire goal of our society should have been to help us "take it easy." Explicitly reflecting Reagan-era individualism, idealism, and ambition, Walter seems to reject this as impractical. "Doesn't anyone give a shit about the rules?" he screams. Yet to rework a key line from the New Testament: "The rules were made for man, not man for the fucking rules." And to paraphrase Voltaire: "The ideal is the enemy of the Dude."[17]

---

17 "The Sabbath was made for man, not man for the Sabbath." *The Bible*, Mark 2:27. And "The ideal is the enemy of the good." Voltaire, "La Bégueule," 1772.

An overemphasis on justice and retribution has resulted in what some pundits call "The Age of Entitlement." This is one of the reasons so many of us feel angry all the time. Yet, followers of the Dude should see those lines drawn in the sand not as provocations, but rather as helpful suggestions. Then we could fulfill the prophetic promise of our Dudeist ancestors and enter a true "Age of Enlightenupment." (See "The Book of Revolutions," page 107.)

As the Dude puts it, "It's just a game, man." He might as well be referring not to the league bylaws, but to life itself.

10. Tie your room together.

Back at his house, we find the Dude not only in his home, but also at home in the world. The initial loss of his rug, which "really tied the room together," is now more clearly put in context. Again and again in the film the Dude retreats to his modest bungalow to rest and recharge from the challenges that the outside world has imposed on him. And each time, he is able to find his center quickly by performing unorthodox meditative routines. In one scene, we see him freshly bathed, performing *tai chi* on his new rug,[18] a White Russian cocktail in hand. "As for compensation," the Dylan theme song to the movie goes,[19] "there's little he would ask." The Dude doesn't ask for much.

---

18 The Dude is even wearing professional *tai chi* shoes, not sneakers, so you know he's really into some kind of Eastern thing.

19 During recording, Dylan would play the song, "The Man In Me," in a completely different tempo than originally agreed upon, which could be part of the reason the song has such an easygoing, improvised feel to it (http://bit.ly/1qQX6e).

Having a cave to retreat to was fundamental to the evolution of human psychology. Regarding *home* as a sacred space instead of just storage for stuff is crucial in helping us deal with the dipshits waiting for us just outside the door. They say your body is your temple, but as temples go, it's a little soft and vulnerable. A modest but quiet space with a good lock on the door is the little compensation we should ask.[20] (See "Fungin' Shway," page 242.)

11. Be there, man.

In literature and films, landlords are usually depicted as greedy and cruel. But the Dude is such a loveable guy that his landlord, Marty, comes to him for support and kindness, even though the Dude is behind on the rent. It seems Marty is an amateur (very amateur) dancer and wants the Dude to come see his "cycle" and give him "notes." Whereas many of us would say yes and then make an excuse for not showing up, we know that the Dude is on the level when he says he'll "be there, man." The Dude may not harbor much of cash value, but clearly he esteems friendships above all else. It is one of the qualities, along with his "well tied together" room, that bestow on him a sort of tattered royalty in a world that would otherwise deny him any stature at all. Yet unlike actual royalty or wealth, friendship and floor coverings are credentials we all can acquire. And at the end of the day, what meaning does social standing have, except in the eyes of our

---

20 Note that while it may seem strange that the Dude's door opens outward (and causes him grief later in the movie), outward-opening doors are actually safer because they're harder to break down from the outside.

compeers? Be there for the world, man, and the world will be there for you. You know, the Royal We.

12. What makes a man? A pair of testicles.

Despite having been given the brush-off by the tycoon Lebowski, a few days later, the Dude is invited back to the mansion. It seems Bunny has been kidnapped, and the old man wants to hire the Dude to help rescue her. "Big" Lebowski even breaks down in tears as he describes his love for the bimbo and wrestles theatrically with the meaning of manhood. So then, his confidence was all a show and actually he's an old softie? Accommodating to a fault (and seduced by the first easy money of his life), the Dude finds his good nature hijacked into helping out.

In this, perhaps the central exchange of the film, Lebowski posits to the Dude, "What makes a man...is it being prepared to do the right thing, no matter what the cost?" to which the Dude flippantly replies, "Sure, that and a pair of testicles." In other words, he doesn't recognize this arbitrary obsession with "manhood" that people still carry around with them in a day and age where physical prowess no longer confers an advantage against wild animals or marauding tribes. Perhaps it is this more than any of his other traits—an unencumbered, nontraditional attitude toward manhood—that so ironically marks him as the "man for his time and place."

As may be appropriate in a film in which the main character's moniker is "the Dude," the meaning of manhood is approached from a variety of angles over the course of the story. The Dude, of course, came of age in a universally long-haired era when masculine ideals were questioned and feminism took root, though that skepticism didn't last long. In fact, if nothing else, the gung-ho '80s seemed to raise the macho modus operandi into a virtual *man*-ifesto. This scene asks us to re-examine the query by addressing a flaw in its construction: What makes a man? A pair of testicles. To maintain any relevance at all, the question should be "what makes a *good* man?" And of course, the answer is, the Dude. He is *good*, man. And thurrah. (See "Subjects Like Women," page 156.)

13. It's like Lenin said, you look for the one who benefits.

Not to split hairs here, but it wasn't Lenin who said that. It was Cicero (Latin: *cui bono*). And though the Dude misquotes him, and uses the line to arrive at the wrong deduction about what happened to Bunny (that she kidnapped herself to scam money out of her foolish husband), it actually proves to be the solution to the entire case. The Dude's fatal flaw is that he, like most of us, tends to place too much trust in the wealthy and powerful. Like your average Pomeranian,[21] we are pack animals who reflexively trust those "bigger" than ourselves.

Had the Dude initially considered "who benefits" from Bunny's disappearance, he should have suspected the Big Lebowski—spouses are normally the first suspects in

---

21 Walter's ex Cynthia's dog isn't a Pomeranian, but a Yorkshire terrier. Just as the marmot in the bathtub is a ferret, and Donny mixes up Lenin and Lennon. Also, Jeffrey Lebowski is not what you call the Dude, his Dudeness, or El Duderino. Perhaps taking potshots at postmodernist linguistic theory, *The Big Lebowski* is full of fluxed-up semiotics. Nearly every scene involves the inability of any of the characters to communicate properly.

criminal investigations. Only, he presumed the old man was on the level and that his tears were genuine. Why? Because "he's fucking loaded."

Though the United States was founded on egalitarian principles, the population of this country is more trusting of the wealthy and powerful than people are in just about any other place on earth. No matter how often it happens, every time a tycoon or politician is discovered to be a fraud, the citizens seem genuinely surprised. Noam Chomsky has ranted endlessly about what a good job the U.S. power structure has done in "manufacturing consent"—that is, in maintaining an illusion of democracy so that people feel in control, even as they're being shepherded slavishly around.

Perhaps we could all benefit a bit more from this healthy distrust of the power structure. Again, this was an idea introduced by the Dude's generation, conveniently forgotten and whitewashed over soon afterward. It may be time to revisit this *a priori* operative skepticism: that power and virtue are fundamentally at odds with each other. After all, this was a major contention of the world's more peaceful religions—Christianity and Buddhism—at least in the original, uncompromised first drafts. Shouldn't it be part of Dudeism as well? (See "Creating a More Dude-ocratic Society," page 129.)

14. The beauty of this plan is its simplicity.

The story moves forward here when Walter unexpectedly joins the Dude in making the million-dollar hand-off to the kidnappers. As a direct result of Walter's naked greed and militaristic mode of operation, it all goes horribly wrong.

This, despite his assertion that "the beauty of this plan is its simplicity. When a plan gets too complex, everything can go wrong. If there's one thing I learned in 'Nam…"

This is a line that would be funny if it weren't so eerily prescient. For decades after the Vietnam War, the United States knew better than to embroil itself in unnecessary overseas combat. That, in fact, was the one thing we supposedly learned in 'Nam—that modern warfare is the very definition of complexity. And everything that can go wrong probably will. When it involves human beings and their conflicting desires, there is no such thing as a simple plan.

Of course, that doesn't stop us from looking for ways to make life simpler. Each of the characters in *The Big Lebowski* boasts his own methods of fashioning the cosmic In-n-Out Burger so that it's easier to swallow: 1) We can buy into a fascist ideology, jamming all the loose laces into little cubbyholes in a giant shoe cabinet that reaches up to the sky (Elder Lebowski, Saddam Hussein, Bush Sr.); 2) we can give up and just cast everything aside as meaningless (the nihilists); 3) we can just follow someone else's dictates and piss on the problem (Treehorn's thugs); 4) we can see every problem as a heroic imperative to attack and rectify at all costs (Walter); 5) we can just avoid the big questions and spend our lives passing the time having fun (Donny, Bunny); or… 6) if we're truly ready to embrace life in its psychedelic, ludicrous, and laughable totality, we can follow the Dude Way. (See "In the Beginning Was the Dude Way," page 10.)

15. No funny shtuff.

Because Walter tries to pull a fast one on the kidnappers, the hand-off is completely botched. You see what happens? Do you see what happens? Trying to scam someone is all too often not worth it. Honesty, humility, and honor may be as unfashionable as the Dude's shoes these days, but they're still the foundation of all successful human relations. As a result of this *funny shtuff,* it seems that the kidnappers are going to kill Bunny.

Morally self-serving Walter, conversely, is unfazed, suggesting they go bowling and forget about the whole thing. He is conveniently confident that Bunny is in on the scam and so is in no danger. Not that he would care if she were, though, having already labeled her a "fucking bitch" and a "whore" and somehow blaming her for the death of his fellow soldiers decades before she was born. Despite any of these thorny ethical issues, Walter is utterly consoled by the fact that they still have the million dollars. Like many in the neoconservative movement his character will ultimately presage, he may speak the currency of values, but when it comes down to it, what he truly values is currency. He says:

16. "Who gets to keep the baksheesh?"

But of course, in the long view, no one does. "Where's the fucking money, Lebowski?" points not to the central mystery of the story, but also to the whole durn human comedy and our investments in the story, feelings, and production value thereof.

17. What would the Dude do?

When the complexities of life bear down upon the Dude, let's be honest, he freaks out a little, reflexively losing his cultivated cool. Like us, he is no saint, is far from superhuman, and so is not likely to be deified the way other prophets of peace sometimes are. But unlike most of us, his un-Dudeness doesn't last long. That's because he employs a simple, time-worn but tested approach to dealing with difficulty. We have to check this with his accountant, of course, but it seems that he has no investments.

Because he has long been accustomed not to expect too much from the world of pain, the Dude is easily and rapidly able to overcome its slings and arrows (and later, scissors and coffee mugs). Shortly after giving an anxious report to the police, the Dude is invited to the house of Lebowski's daughter Maude for a *tete-a-tete* regarding the kidnapping. And he's pretty cool and collected by then, mixing cocktails, being fatuous, maybe even flirting with her a little. And then, on the ride home, the whole disaster is already *fuggedaboudit*. Commiserating with Maude's Italian limo driver,[22] the Dude says "I was feeling really shitty earlier in the day; I'd lost a little money. I was down in the dumps... Fuck it!"

---

22 Though close-cropped comedian Dom Irrera plays Tony, the role was originally meant to go to an actor "about the same age, from whose livery cap a ponytail emerges," according to the Coens' published version of the screenplay. This suggests a closer cultural and sartorial compeer of the Dude. But then, it wasn't necessary. The Dude relates to everybody.

18. Can't be worrying about that shit. Life goes on, man.

As we just said, the Dude is neither saintly nor superhuman. But he is a sort of superhee-ro, with a mighty and highly useful superpower—to take it easy where others might take umbrage. It's a power available to all of us if we can just follow in the Dude's jellysteps.[23] No radioactive sloth or koala need bite us to turn us into Duderman, just an appreciation for the beauty of simplicity. What's more, the only reason he is thrown into a panic again and again from here on in is because he strayed from the original "simple plan," the one that had served him so well for the last forty-something years.

19. That's just the stress talking.

Moments after telling Maude's limo driver that he "can't be worried about that shit, life goes on," life does, in fact, go on and provides new shit to worry about. Dropped off at his house by Maude's driver, he's pushed into another Lebowski limo, that of her father. As expected, the Dude is accused of stealing the million dollars instead of handing it off to the kidnappers, despite his feeble protestations that he dropped off the money. The Dude is fibbing here, and perhaps this should concern us, but at this point he is of the opinion that no one has been hurt. But the stakes are raised when he's presented with a human toe, purported to have been cut from the foot of Lebowski's wife Bunny—a consequence of his failure to "achieve the modest task which was [his] charge."

---

23 The Dude's jelly sandals were Jeff Bridges' own. He also wore them in *White Squall* in 1996. Similarly, the Japanese baseball shirt was also his own. He wore that as well in *The Fisher King* (1991). The Dude obliges!

Every superhero has his weakness. Whereas superman has kryptonite, the Dude has his conscience. It's not easy being nonchalant and easygoing when you care about your fellow humans and someone's "life is in your hands." As the only character blessed (or saddled) with compassion and conscience, the Dude is the only one with real cause to worry about Bunny's well-being. It would be so much easier to "take it easy" if he were truly as apathetic as his adversaries presume.

Flung into another funk, the Dude plies Walter for help and advice at a coffeehouse but is met with nothing but aloof disparagement. "That's not her toe," Walter jeers, brushing off the gambit as the work of "fucking amateurs." The Dude loses his cool at this point, concerned that the kidnappers will not only kill Bunny, but will kill him as well. This prompts Walter to try something more soothing. "That's just the stress talking, Dude," he says. It is a ridiculous and insensitive remark, but true to some degree. So what does the Dude do? He skee-doodles. The stress needs to stop talking.

20. This affects all of us, Dude.

The Dude storms out of the coffeehouse and Walter calls after him, "This affects all of us, Dude!" Walter is, of course, referring to his "basic freedom" to holler in the coffeehouse, but this, of course, is Walter's own "stress talking"—a morbid and monomaniacal creature that truly never shuts the fuck up.

As we mentioned before, it's been shown repeatedly by scientific experiment that mood (bad or good) is far more contagious than any germ-based disease. The way we act around others influences them and spreads out throughout society like ripples in a pond. Though the Dude may not gen-erate wealth and innovation, which might contribute to the comforts of civilization, his supernaturally positive outlook and easygoing manner are arguably just as influential to society as a whole. Whereas Walter's exercising of his "free-dom" to shout in a coffeehouse will have negative repercus-sions that will likely be passed on by everyone in the room to their friends and families, the Dude spares them all his own negative vibe by getting out of the place and getting his head together. Sometimes the villain we have to save people from is ourselves. To the bath cave, Duderman!

21. Shomer Shabbos!

As we've pointed out, the Dude generally values rest above activity. Walter, as an observant convert to Judaism, also believes in the sanctity of rest—the Jews, after all, invent-ed the Sabbath. But how enjoyable and salutary can rest be when it's forced and only comes once a week? Rest is restor-ative; it's a drug that keeps our bodies and minds limber. Like physical medicine, if it's administered at the wrong time, it can't effectively treat the disease of *dis-ease*.

As opposed to Shomer Shabbos, *Duder Shabbos* is prac-ticed far more regularly. At least once a day, if not more, a true follower of the Dude will set aside time to say "Fuck it" and do fuck all. Whether that entails meditating on the rug, or hanging out in the bath listening to whale sounds, or just enjoying the occasional acid flashback, it is imperative that we find time to fill with emptiness. It is at our own peril that we fail to recognize our need for nothing.

As if putting his super Duder power to the test once again, the Dude doesn't take long to get the stress to stop talking. *Shut the fuck up, stressy!* It is in the very next scene that we find him relaxing in the bath with a meditation tape of whale sounds playing in the background and melting candles flickering about the rim of the tub. He languidly finishes off a flaming roach of soothing dope.

The universe seems to reward him in his efforts to cool down by sending a message through his answering machine—his stolen car has been recovered! "Far out," the Dude coos, until a crashing noise from the other room indicates that a whole new goon squad has broken in unwelcomed to his pad.

22. Don't drag this negative energy into the tournament.

Again, the Dude comports himself admirably under the circumstances. After his door is broken open, and his answering machine has been smashed with a cricket bat,[24] he coolly leans out of the tub to see who's there and calls out, "Hey man, this is a *private* residence." Then, when the cadre of three leather-clad nihilists storm into the bathroom with a wild ferret on a leash, he nods appreciatively, "Nice marmot." It is not until the crazed animal is thrown into the water to

---

24 Germans and other continental Europeans don't generally play cricket. But the cricket bat clearly suggests a foreign and unwelcome version of the all-American baseball bat depicted on the Dude's shirt in an earlier scene, though held, oddly, by a Japanese baseball player. The whole notion of American national identity is hilariously mangled in *The Big Lebowski*, suggesting a sort of loss of the clear parameters of an earlier era.

thrash around his crotch region that he starts to scream in terror. Some people have low boiling points. The Dude is such a chilled fellow that even when confronted with the rudest behavior, it takes nothing less than the threat of genital mutilation to bring him to simmer.

In the next scene, the Dude again comically supplicates his powerful, stern, and pathologically unconcerned friend Walter for help. As they sit in the bowling alley and the Dude shares his worry that the nihilists will cut off his "chonsson" if he doesn't give them the million dollars he lost, Walter says, "You've got to buck up. You can't drag this negative energy into the tournament." Like most people, Walter can be quite the Dudeist when it comes to other people's problems.

The Dude does his best, but even he can't let the situation slide. "Fuck the tournament, and fuck you, Walter!" he wails. It is the first time we see the Dude truly vulnerable. Darkness has "warshed over." In other words, he is on the brink of letting "this negative energy" defeat him. All is lost! Remember that the Dude's quest is not for a grail, after all, or money, or even his ratty old rug. His mythological "hero's journey" is to remain utterly lazy and relaxed even when the world makes it virtually impossible for him to do so.

It is in this *dark tookus of the soul* moment that the mythical, mysterious, and ludicrously mustachioed narrator, the Stranger, finally appears to provide sage and timely advice. Like some kind of Okie Wan Kenobi, the Stranger plays mentor to our floundering hero when he needs it most, sympathizing and bucking him up the way Walter can't. As the "Tumbling Tumbleweeds" song from the opening credits fades in, the camera pulls back to reveal Sam Elliott in appropriately anachronistic cowboy garb, seated next to the Dude, ordering a *sarsaparilla*.

What the fuck is this, man? Some sort of acid flashback? In fact it is, of a kind. The cowboy is a mythical American messenger, like the gods of Olympus, or the angels of the Bible, wandering in from an old Marlboro ad or spaghetti western or peyote postscript, to bring a message from the great beyond, assuring and fortifying this guardian of the *Wilde* West Dude tradition in his darkest hour. And what is his message?

23. "Sometimes you eat the bar [bear]. And sometimes, the bar, wal, he eats you."[25]

The Dude shrugs it off. "What is that, some kind of Eastern thing?" he grumbles. And of course it could be, though the cowboy demurs. We in the West spent the latter part of the disastrous 20th century looking eastward for inspiration because it seemed as if our Occidental canon had failed us. And yet the idea that the West is about achievement while the East is about contemplation is just a convenient fiction for target marketers. It may be true that Western religion and philosophy have created more anxiety on the whole than their Eastern counterparts, but the impulse toward moral indolence and meditative passivism has been at least as highly revered and developed

---

25 The Stranger pronounces the word "bar," but he is saying "bear" in an antiquated rustic American dialect. Though there is some disagreement about this among Lebowski fans, the theme song from the 1960s Daniel Boone TV series proves that "bar" was an acceptable pronunciation of "bear." See: http://bit.ly/dYnizn.

by European scholars as it has by Asian ones. If there's anything the Eastern "side" of civilization has done better, it's to organize those impulses effectively into a common system of technique, and to officially sanction them as an "answer for everything." Oh, and also, as is the case with Indian yogis, sometimes they even do tattoo it on their foreheads.

24. Dig styles.

Though the Dude has bigger burgers to fry at the moment than making new friends with oddly dressed strangers, he is appropriately cordial to the man, so much so that when the Stranger offers him a compliment ("I dig your style, Dude"), the Dude cheers up noticeably and responds in kind. In truth, the Dude digs all sorts of styles. It is no mean feat, especially when there are so many "styles" evident in a tolerant modern civilization, so many of which run contrary to our own.

There's a principle in many religions (e.g. Judaism, Islam, Hinduism, Norse Paganism) that one should always dig the style of strangers lest they be gods in disguise, dropping in unannounced to test our moral resolve. It's a silly and somewhat circuitously self-serving notion, of course, but it probably had a profound effect on human relations. Welcoming strangers and digging their style, no matter how bizarre they might seem, is the grease that makes the wheels of civilization turn. Sadly, these "manners" sometimes appear quaint and laughably old-fashioned today. Radio shock jocks, sensationalist press, harried life schedules, and the commercial triumph of "fashion" have helped instill a knee-jerk tendency to criticize and prejudge people without giving them a chance to show their Dude colors. And knee jerks make jerk-offs of all of us.

There may be a semblance of truth to the old religious superstition though. We should treat strangers with kindness and accommodation, but not because they are gods who will punish us if we don't. We should be dude to them because they are reflections of ourselves—just like the Dude's face in the "Are You a Lebowski Achiever?" mirror is an oblique reflection of the millionaire. But achievement can go fuck itself (and often does). It is only our kindness that will be reflected back outward and onward, down through the generations, across the sands of time. The man for our time and place is the one who can give anyone the time of day, no matter how rough a time they may be personally having themselves. Everyone we encounter deserves to be treated as sacred because with a few negligible exceptions, the entire world is composed of strangers. It's got that whole sacred cowboy thing goin' on.

25. This is a complicated case. Lotta ins and outs. Lotta what-have-yous. Lotta strands in old Duder's head.

Called back to Maude's loft, the Dude finally loses his cool with her. Like everyone else in the film other than the Dude, she stubbornly believes that she's got everything figured out already.

It takes a big man to admit he's wrong. But it takes a far bigger man to admit he doesn't have any fucking clue in the first place. Of all the claims leveled against religion, surely the worst is its outright, blatant, and unapologetic arrogance.

To claim to "know" how the world came into existence could easily be diagnosed as acute megalomania if it weren't such a universal malady. It seems that human beings would rather give a wrong answer to an impossible question than say, "I don't know, sir." Am I wrong? Okay then.

Though most of the characters he encounters in the film pretend to have everything figured out, the Dude labors under no such delusions of omniscience. What's wrong with the world? What's right with it? What really matters? The Dude makes no such elaborate, outrageous territorial claims to some sort of philosophical high ground. At several points throughout the film he happily admits his ignorance outright. While Walter is 100 percent certain that Bunny kidnapped herself, and Maude states that Bunny is "most certainly" the perpetrator of the scam, and the Big Lebowski pretends to be assured that it is the Dude who is "unrepentantly" at fault here, the Dude is the only one holding fast to the idea that the whole thing might be more complex...it might not be such a...a...you know?

Critics of the Dude make a lot of hoo-hah about how inept the Dude is as a private eye, how he can't manage to put a coherent thought or theory together until the very end of the film. What they overlook is that coherence is the opposite of creativity. What's the point in being coherent until the parts of an argument actually begin to cohere? Until then, the Dude with his jazzy, roundabout mode of expression and investigation is exactly the right type of existential detective for these complex, convoluted times—arguably even more so than Douglas Adams' existential detective Dirk Gently,[26] who stated in particularly Dudeish fashion, "Capital letters were always the best way of dealing with things you didn't have a good answer to." Like Dirk Gently, the Dude doesn't always have answers, but he has lots of strands waiting to be woven. That's both far-out and far-sighted.

26. Do, do, do, look out your back door.

After visiting Maude for the second time, and having her "not fucking listen" to a word he says and insist that he see her doctor, the Dude drives home in a good mood. He's listening to Creedence Clearwater Revival, smoking a joint, and drinking a beer. Though he's breaking several laws simultaneously, we enjoy watching him enjoy himself—it comes so preternaturally to him, after all. Watching the Dude enjoy himself is like watching Superman shoot laser beams out of his eyes.

There is some debate over why the Dude is so happy at this point—after all, it's likely that minutes earlier the doctor stuck his finger up the Dude's anus to extract a sperm sample (we figure this out later). However, to conflate his good cheer with a clinical ejaculation delivered by a middle-aged male doctor surely strains at the limits of the Dude's accommodating aspect.

Why is the Dude happy? A better question would be: Why are we surprised at unconditional cheer? And why don't

---

26 Douglas Adams' character Dirk Gently was born with the name Svlad Cjelli. It seems that Eastern Europeans have cornered the market when it comes to wacky and philosophical detective work. They also don't like to use their given names.

we experience it more often ourselves? There is so much even in the most miserable life to appreciate. After all, the song playing in his car is "Lookin' Out My Back Door" and it concerns an imaginary parade of bizarre visions passing in front of songwriter John Fogerty as he lets his mind wander. It is one of the few classic rock songs that celebrate not just having sex and its variants, but the salutary effects that imagination and meditation can have on the harried soul. The "back door" in the song surely leads to the unconscious. Then again, who knows, it might just refer to his anus. (See "Dudeitation," page 199.)

27. A few burgers, some beers, some laughs. Our troubles are over, Dude.

Shortly thereafter, partially because of the pot and beer, the Dude crashes his car. As he struggles to get out of the damaged vehicle, he is surprised to find a crumpled-up piece of homework wedged in the seat. It is a clue to who stole his vehicle, and presumably made off with the million dollars! In a traditional film, this would be a turning point. But in *The Big Lebowski*, it's just another hilarious wrong turn.

With greater investigative resources at his disposal, Walter dons a business suit and takes up the case—that is, figuring out whose homework it is, and where he lives. Pleased that they are on the verge of getting the money back, Walter says their "troubles are over" in anticipation of the merriment they will soon enjoy after they're finished suffering through Marty's dance quintet, his cycle, or as Walter puts it, his "what-have-you."

It doesn't come to pass, of course. The Coens don't allow the Dude more than a brief moment of satisfaction or hope before *pulling the rug* out from under him again and again. And yet the "burgers, beers, and laughs" line points to the very meat and potatoes of the movie: There never were any fucking troubles, Dude! They threw out a ringer for a ringer. In other words, all the troubles in the film were of the characters' own making. And any real pleasure to be found in life could have been obtained cheaply from burgers, beers, and laughs. And this, before the vaunted million dollars ever entered their lives. Let's not forget, let's *NOT* forget...to not forget this.

Just because we're *ennuied* doesn't make us saps.

28. We've got a language problem here.

After driving Dude's rapidly deconstructing car to his house in the Valley, Walter and Dude enter the alleged thief's house and confront the 15-year-old kid by thrusting his homework at him (in a plastic baggie, for dramatic effect), demanding an answer. And then, the incredible happens. In a film where all the characters "blather" without end, the kid who contains the answer to the whole thing (parts anyway) won't say a peep while they're doing business here!

For a man accustomed to using language (as well as handguns) in order to dominate other people, stonewalling is an inexcusable infraction of the rules of engagement— remember that, for Walter, nihilism is worse than nazism because even an evil argument is preferable to none at all. Little Larry's refusal to play by Walter's rules naturally drives Walter insane. "We've got a language problem here!"

he shouts, before heading outside to exact punishment by smashing the brand new Corvette that he thinks Larry procured with a portion of the million dollars. Echoed here is the cruelly delivered threat to *Cool Hand Luke* by his prison warden: "What we have here is a failure to communicate." In other words: The problem is that you refuse to let me dominate you. And in fact, Little Larry is foreshadowing a later scene in which the Dude does exactly the same thing. Little Larry may in fact be a Little Lebowski on the way.

In many ways, the entire movie can be seen as an exegesis on "the language problem" Walter objects to. Though Walter resents the fact that Larry won't reply to him, he himself doesn't ever allow anyone to disagree with him. What's the use of engaging with someone who has already drawn his lines in the sand? Though he may supposedly be "a fucking dunce," Little Larry has sized up his predicament and reflexively determined that he must employ *Dude-jitsu* in dealing with his adversaries. It is a mute echo of the Dude's principled "Fuck it" in front of Lebowski. (See "This Agression Will Not Stand," page 206.)

Perhaps it is due to the fact that he has been so expertly out-Duded, that here we see the Dude for the first time utterly out of his element. Certainly this is his most un-Dude point in the film; he sinks so low as to curse out the youth in front of his dying father, and even maintains that they "know" Larry took the money! Dude, you're being verrry un-Dude. Thankfully, this brief Dude-parture doesn't last for long.

As modern politics and Gallup polls prove, very few people budge from their tightly guarded positions, nor even listen to the arguments of others. As Steven Covey puts it in

The Seven Habits of Highly Effective People, few people actually listen to each other. To employ "emphatic" listening is to understand that communication is far more complex than just a series of signs, signals, and symbols. If someone isn't prepared to listen, why waste your energy? As a Dudeist version of that cheesy pop song might go: "You say it best/When you say nothing/Stonewall."

Yet to understand language as a fluid, creative process that must be played with and batted around is the first step toward being more Dude. No cunning linguist, but a cuddly one, the Dude plays with words and phrases like they're part of some crazy game, echoing things he's overheard from other characters in the film, always reinventing ideas to suit new situations. Other characters utilize language and conversation aggressively. For example, Walter steers every discussion toward the Vietnam War, Maude uses language as a method of social stratification, and Jackie Treehorn employs conversation merely as a tool of distraction and manipulation. But the Dude uses it to seek synthesis. By borrowing ideas and phrases from other characters, he weaves a sort of epic stoner poetry from the threads of other people's assertions.[27] (See "Self-Help Chopperin' In," page 177.)

---

27 Of course, it's not just the Dude who repeats lines from other characters. In The Big Lebowski universe, certain phrases and words like "Chinaman," "abide," "parlance of our times," "where's the money, Lebowski?" "this aggression will not stand," "no funny stuff," "your answer for everything," "nothing is fucked," "have it your way, Dude," and more float around and inhabit characters' brains like spirits. Each time a line is repeated from another context it helps to illuminate just how much we are products of our culture, rather than the other way around. Nevertheless, the Dude seems to navigate this stream of weird clichés with more finesse than the others, employing them gingerly and at arm's length.

29. Jerk off by hand.

Few of us might remember that the early 1990s were filled with a brave new hope that technology might save us from one of the most problematic issues facing mankind: getting laid. After all, in the developed world, we can get housing and food and diversion, but experiencing orgasm when administered by someone else is still a challenge for most people. Thus it wasn't long after the dawn of computer porn that people envisaged a time in the near future when our sexual needs would be easily satisfied by "virtual sexuality." Soon we were all going to be fucking virtual partners without having to buy them dinner or respect them in the morning, and no one would care! Johnson? What do you need that for, Dude?

This brief flirtation with high-technonanism is captured neatly by the Coen Brothers in the exchange the Dude has with Jackie Treehorn after being invited to his "unspoiled pad" to discuss the matter of Bunny's disappearance. Porn king Treehorn laments the fact that video technology has made it easy for "amateurs" to enter a world of porn. Like any savvy capitalist, he hopes to maintain his status by developing ever newer and more robust technologies to better administer to the ancient and much-loved pastime of rubbing one's genitals while pretending someone else is. But the Dude sees through the charade. "I still jerk off manually," he says. And why not? Why should he pay for something he can do himself?

The technological world we live in has not replaced the biological one. To some degree it has enhanced it, but to a degree it's also damaged it. Our daily obsession with gizmos and internet spectacle has surely made a dent in the human condition, even as it's extended it. You know what I'm trying to say. Are you ready to be fucked, man?

The Dude is no technophobe (he sort of digs the beeper and huge telephone, and enjoys driving around and partaking of modern pharmaceuticals), but he is also precociously wary of the dawn of the "technological revolution." The point, as he seems to understand it, is to be extended by it, not dented. Look for the one who benefits: *Cui boner*. In many cases it is not we who are aided by technology, but rather the companies who are desperately trying to seduce us with their "objects like women."

30. The brain is the biggest erogenous zone.

Though the Dude replies to Jackie Treehorn's statement about the brain with a dismissive "on you maybe," this is in fact a fully Dudeist approach to life. The Dude is no swinging-dick womanizer or puffed-up macho man. The Dude balls, but the dude minds as well. It is for this reason that he realizes that he doesn't hold "the smut business" in high regard. His imagination is all he needs to find a more natural, holistic avenue to self-satisfaction. *Do, do, do, look out your back door.* Don't, don't, don't look at too much internet porn.

As if in answer to the implication that he doesn't need Jackie's "business" and can make it up himself, thank you, we get a glimpse into the Dude's rich, sexy, and surreal "life of the mind." After Treehorn drugs his White Russian, the movie ushers in one of the wildest dream sequences in cinematic history.

31. Just drop in to see what condition your condition is in.

Though the 20th century was hallmarked by "big ideas," not all of those ideas were bad. One of the most famous was the notion that there was more to our consciousness than what we were strictly conscious of. The rise of the psychological sciences paid testament to the fact that "this whole fucking thing" might be bigger and more complex than we originally imagined. And though Sigmund Freud is now pilloried for focusing too much on sex, aggression, and the subliminal (vagina), there's still a lot to be said for the power, depth, and breadth of the subconscious mind.

Is our subconscious a method for dealing with conflict? Is it a vestigial leftover from a biological inheritance? Is it a way of working out problems on another level? It don't matter to the Dudeist. As long as it's "fucking interesting" and "keeps our mind limber," we'll take whatever it serves up. Just like his approach in dealing with the conscious world, the Dude's approach to dreams and imagination might be to respect its more interesting elements without getting too hung up on what it all might mean. In order to strengthen the bridge between the conscious and subconscious, a fair bit of daily "checking in" is in order. Dudeitation, baths, quietude, and "tying the room together" are all ways to ensure that we're well aware of our condition so that we can defend against the conditioning of others.

32. Don't treat objects like women, man.

After the Dude wakes up in the Malibu police chief's office, he finds that Jackie Treehorn called the cops because he was being "abusive" at his party. Still under the influence of the drugged cocktail, Dude mumbles, "Jackie Treehorn treats objects like women, man." As we alluded to above, what sort of a Freudian slip could better sum up the fetishization and sexualization of technology during the ensuing decade and into the 2000s?

Several times in the film the Dude seems like an accidental prophet. Just as he saw where our aggression was heading by dating the check September 11, 1991, as he watched Bush declare war on Iraq in the opening scene, so does his limber mind intuit what's in store for the world when it comes to sex and commerce. In 1990 (when the film was meant to take place[28]) and even in 1998 (when it was filmed), the world still had no idea of the degree to which people would come to "treat objects like women," that is, as objects of desire. Remember that until the iMac came out in 1998, most gadgets were strictly coveted for their utilitarian economics, not for their "sexy" ergonomics. How's the smut business, Jobsey? These days, it's everywhere. Only the four unflinchingly ironic eyes of the Coen Brothers would see that a fetish for gadgetry is a variety of porn in its own right, not just a channel for its

---

28 Though the Dude dates his check September 11, 1991, Bush delivered his "aggression will not stand" speech in the summer of 1990. Either the Dude has postdated his check by a year or so, or in addition to not knowing if it's a weekday, he also doesn't know what year it is. And that's cool. That's cool.

dissemination. And that's cool. That's cool. But the dangers of techno-lust are the same as the dangers of porn: namely, a disconnect from a more innate way of living, one which tends to make humans feel healthy and happy.

33. Keep your mind limber.

The Dude returns to his home to find that Jackie Treehorn had it ransacked, looking for the missing million dollars. But at long last, the Dude gets his day in the sun—or moon, rather. Maude is there waiting for him and invites him to engage in a "natural, zesty enterprise." You mean, coitus? Oh, yes, Mr. Lebowski.

It is in the cozy, hazy, post-coital dog-day afterglow that the Dude finally pieces together the mystery of the whole kidnapping case. The yin and the yang come together to make everything wholey. The Dude's fluid, alternately aggressive and receptive nature lent him the flexibility to "get down to cases." It increases the chances of conception. Though he claims that it's "a strict drug regimen" that keeps his mind limber enough to figure out this "complex case," we know that the drugs aren't mere dope or drink. Nope, the Dude is all fucked up on life, and it is the resulting "limberal" thinking that allows him to see the forest for the trees in a way that is impossible for everyone else in the film, addicted to sobriety as they are. (See "Duderinos Unanimous," page 192.)

34. You're goddamn right, we're living in the past.

When Maude tells the Dude that her father doesn't have any money of his own and in fact has been a lifelong failure in business and everything else, the Dude realizes that he has been played for a fool. There never was any fucking money! The Big Lebowski embezzled the money and gave the Dude an empty suitcase to give to the kidnappers. Suddenly, the world has gone downright Biblical: The meek shall be exalted, the mountain shall be laid low. As the Dude is raised up, the Big Lebowski is revealed to be puny. And also, the lion gets in bed with the lamb. And soon, we'll happen to know that there's a Little Lebowski to be begat, down through the generations.

Moreover, as if to emphasize the Old Testament nature of all this new shit, the secret of Walter's Jewishness is subsequently addressed. And it is here that the whole scope and scale of the film is illuminated. As it turns out, *The Big Lebowski* is even bigger and wider and deeper than we could have imagined.

Because his ailing car won't make it all the way to Pasadena, the Dude calls on Walter again, demanding that he give him a ride even if it is Shabbos, the Jewish day of rest. Walter obliges, but complains that it's not really an emergency worthy of his breaking strict 3,000-year old laws. Here the Dude finally hits Walter where he is weakest, pointing out that he's not really Jewish, that he converted to please his ex-wife and only holds onto the old religion as a way to maintain a connection with his loss.

It's easy at this point to see this as just a funny little bit of character development—that Walter's obsession with Judaism is just an arbitrary reflection of how sad he still is about a five-year-old divorce. But in a movie in which the Dude is dressed like a Biblical Jesus and upholds the

Nazarene's moral code; in which there actually is a debased character called "The Jesus"; in which Persian carpets, Babylonian ziggurats,[29] Hebrew traditions, and the Canaanite landscape of Los Angeles play so prominently, it's hard not to see this not only as a means to "wrap 'er all up" but to "wrap up" the last "3,000 years of beautiful tradition" as well.

Just as the Dude is reluctant to blindly ride the "wave of the future," rejecting much of the code of progress, so is he acutely aware of the crippling gravity of history. Ideology in all forms is a pernicious combination of "living in the fucking past" and anxious attempts to ride the "wave of the future." Like many a popular self-help guru, the Dude spends most of his time living in his "time and place," and borrowing only cautiously from other time zones, lest they bump him into a higher existential tax bracket.

Thus it is here that the Coen Brothers provide the widest of all angles in the entire sweep of their cinematic oeuvre. In having Walter scream, "3,000 years of beautiful tradition, from Moses to Sandy Koufax...You're goddamn right I'm living in the past!" the breadth of what they're imparting appears fairly staggering. It seems that, like Walter, we too are living in the past, attached to a worldview we have grown apart from. It's all a part of our sick civilization thing!

---

29 In the second dream sequence, the bowling shoe cabinet that reaches up to the sky and up to the moon behind Saddam Hussein is a clear reference to the myth of the Babylonian ziggurats, which progress-obsessed men built in order to produce a "stairway to heaven." As a result of which, God got angry and made it impossible for man to communicate and get along by creating "the language problem." Do you see what happens, *Domini*?

Aside from minor modifications, America and a large part of Western civilization still operates from an ancient mind-set derived from the earliest beginnings of Western culture, one that is rather outdated and arguably maladapted for our time and place. We must ultimately move on and leave it behind if we're ever to enter the New Dude Age.

35. The whole concept abates.

In many ways, the Dude is like the original Jesus, who briefly got his day in the sun and then was buried and resurrected as someone rather different. Though there are several pretenders to the throne, the Dude is the only "true Jesus" in the film. Donny's sacrificial death places him high in the running, and the Jesus has the name and the Latin pedigree, but it is only the Dude who embodies the reformist attitude that the Church never allowed to come to full flower. While St. Paul and the Council of Nicea refashioned the sage of the sagebrush as a god, the Dude's humanistic spirit slouched down through the ages, westward the wagons, through new Bethlehems, ultimately ending up on Venice Beach waiting to be reborn.[30]

The Dude represents a possible break with this crusty old tradition, incorporating the best of the Axial Age philosophy and freeing it from the fascist imperatives that our civilization perniciously added later. The whole Judeo-Christian concept abates because it doesn't adequately represent its

---

30 "The darkness drops again but now I know/That twenty centuries of stony sleep/Were vexed to nightmare by a rocking cradle,/And what rough beast, its hour come round at last,/Slouches towards Bethlehem to be born?" William Butler Yeats, *The Second Coming*

original virtues. And as a result, it continues to throw out ringers for ringers.

So what, then, are our Biblical "dirty undies"? The linear, progressive notion of life and time; the necessity of justice and retribution; the need for an overarching meaning and explanation for everything; the myth of the hero; the idea of an end of history and a grand reckoning; the promise of a great reward for toeing the line until then; the sense of tribal "specialness"; and perhaps most outdated of all, the fucking TOE—the idea that we can ever arrive at a stone-chiseled "theory of everything."

There's more to this than our sick civilization thing, however: We're still living in the past biologically. So we have to learn to stop teasing the monkey. As an example, the Dude stands out as the only character who can properly control his limbic system. Everyone else is buffeted around by their emotions, yawping like so many marmots or Pomeranians, addicted to drugs of their own production. Walter's anger, as it turns out, has very little to do with Vietnam. Every time he blows his top in the film, it comes on the heels of a mention of his ex-wife or other unfaithful women ("You're entering a world of pain!" "Shomer Shabbos!" "V. I. Lenin!"). Walter is not angry after all—he's just down in the dumps. That's just the *depression* talking.

The Dude is radically progressive, then, not in a political sense, but in an existential one. His character represents both a break with the emotional imperatives of biology and society and with millennia-old ideology that is long past its sell-by date. Whereas everyone else is miserable and unful-filled and lost because they think they need a "direction," the

Dude shows us a way to be "at home" in the world even without a destination in mind. Like an old Taoist monk, he goes with the flow even as he remains utterly still.

After this revelation, Walter and the Dude arrive in Pasadena and find that Bunny has returned to the mansion with all her toes intact. Not only was there no money, but there was never was any fucking kidnapping. Everything's a travesty, man! And the no-longer-so-Big Lebowski is unrepentant as he is revealed. He too is shown to be as miserable and overcompensating as Walter, sobbing on the floor, mourning a life not yet lived despite its approaching end. It is a ghost of Christmas or a picture of Dorian Gray or a Marty McFly moment of redemption for the Dude, affirming once and for all that it is this Small Lebowski who deserves our admiration. That's terrific because, in most cases, we are *that* Lebowski.

36. Get out of this thing cheap.

According to the original listed runtime of the film (98 minutes), the movie should be over now. But there are still 20 minutes to go! Now that's fucking interesting, man. Is there an unspoken message here? Perhaps it's to underscore the fact that the conventional part of the story should be seen as separate from what it's really all about.

Back among the flock of holy bowlers, Walter is holding forth as usual, blathering about how the Gulf War is all about oil, comparing it unfavorably to the Vietnam War—"now that's fucking combat." On the heels of this statement, he and the Dude and Donny face real-life combat out in the parking lot. The nihilists still want the money, and they're prepared to "fucks you up" to get it. Though they will settle for pocket change, Walter adheres stubbornly to his 3,000-year-old Code of Hammurabi tradition of "desert warfare" rather than adopting a more flexible attitude. The Dude insists, "C'mon man, we're getting out of this thing cheap!" but they go to battle anyway. Walter vanquishes his enemy, but Donny dies in the melee—from a heart attack. In a war between fanaticism and nihilism, the naive pawns among us will find themselves batted around like bowling pins.

Delivering a eulogy on the bluffs south of Los Angeles overlooking the ocean, Walter tries to wrap up the life of his friend Donny, but just as the Coens do with the story itself, he too will fail. There is nothing in the film to indicate that weedy, pale Donny is a surfer, and his best friends don't know how he wanted to be disposed of.[31] Walter dumps the cremains from a cheap coffee can and the ash blows back in their faces.

This is what our lives amount to in the end: a silly comedy of errors in which we aren't even truly known or understood by our closest compeers. Sadly, real life does not wrap up as neatly as a typical Hollywood movie. Yet from the Dudeist point of view, this is no great tragedy.

Ultimately we all get out of this thing cheap. Regardless of all that we might acquire or achieve in life, we are all piss-poor in death, and recognizing that might allow us to recognize the priceless value of life. Our lives are our only true asset, and aspiring toward greatness, or power, or glory, or

---

31 Does it reveal anything when we find out that Donny is Greek (his last name is Karabatsos)? One wonders—in a film where "Jesus" is a vicious and deranged pedophile, might it not mean something that a character who represents the highest peak of ancient civilization is presented as a feeble dimwit? Well dude, we just don't know.

gold utterly misses the point of what we're supposed to do with our seed capital. Living is the end in itself. It is the greatest art imaginable, and everything that helps us appreciate it is an investment in our modest temporary checking account and the club of value.

37. Fuck it, Dude, let's go bowling.

And so, having accomplished little and lost plenty, Walter says to his best pal, "Fuck it, Dude, let's go bowling." It is both a surrender and an embrace. There is no sport better suited than bowling to help visualize the nature and art of living. It is both an utterly pointless endeavor and an utterly beautiful pastime. It requires no special ability or conditioning. It is profoundly social. And even a child can do it.[32]

It is this: Take something heavy and unwieldy and set it in motion. Try to let it flow with balance and between a tension of opposites. Sit down and rest. Then stand up and try again. *Whoo!* Mark it lazy eight, Dude: that is to say, infinity. We are all of us dead in the water.

38. The Dude abides.

To wrap things all up, or to make an attempt at least, our cowboy narrator shows up once again. We still don't know why he's there, but we like the fact that he is. He's a comforting presence. Without him we might not have recognized how important the Dude actually is, might have laughed him off as a mere buffoon. But by placing the Dude in context, priming us to understand that he's not just a man, but that

---

32 It is also one of the oldest, if not *the* oldest, commonly played sport in the world. 5,000 years of Dudeyful tradition.

he's "the man for his time and place" who is "takin 'er easy for us sinners," the Stranger achieves the modest task that was his charge, and he can get back on that suitably high horse, rambling further on down the trail.

This, of course, is the reason mankind stubbornly adheres to the idea of religion or God, and avatars like Jesus, Krishna, the Buddha. There's something undeniably comforting in believing there's a right way to do things, something prefigured into the tapestry of the universe, the rug that ties everything together. And that there are men for their time and place that can best exemplify how we ourselves might "fit right in there." Whether these beliefs are true or not, mankind is in desperate need of them. However, after 3,000 years of beautiful tradition, might it not be high time to look toward another bearded, misunderstood monk who drinks carefully from the sacred beverage of half-and-half?

When the film's folksy narrator wishes the Dude good luck, our hee-ro says, "Well, you know, the Dude abides," and the Stranger "takes comfort in that." But "Dude" has already been established in the film as a non-personal noun, as a state of being, as in the *Dude* and the *un-Dude*. "The Dude abides," therefore, doesn't just refer to this one person in this one place at this one time, but to an eternal principle of Dudeism. Down through the ages. Across the sands of time. It perseveres as it plays. It takes it easy for us sinners. It always has.[33]

---

33 Today, "abide" is a word most commonly used by Christians to describe their loyalty to Jesus Christ. The Dude even adopts a shlumpy Christ-like stance with beers in hand as he says his signature line. While technically it's just an echo of the other Lebowski's statement that "I will not abide another toe," it's also got some of that olde-tyme religious flavor to it. Just like that good sarsaparilla.

The Stranger then says, "Welp, that about wraps 'er up." But of course, on face value, it absolutely does not. The Dude doesn't get his rug back and we don't know if he and Walter win the tournament. We don't even know for sure if Lebowski stole the money, and if he did, whether it was ever returned. So many of the strands in old Dude's head are still loose, flapping in the wind like the frayed ends of a half-woven rug. But then, why should *The Big Lebowski* be neatly wrapped up when life itself is not?

That's the way the whole durn human comedy keeps perpetuatin' itself. The story's ludicrous. But it's a good story. Don'tcha think? Forget about the fucking TOE. Were you listening to the Dude's story? Sometimes there's a frame of reference. It's the worldview for its time and place. And that's also the Dude's, in *The Big Lebowski*. Abide by this.

II

Wiser Fellers Than Ourselves— Dudeist History

GREAT DUDES IN HISTORY

What makes a Great Dude?

Is it being prepared to always take 'er easy, whatever the cost? Are Great Dudes only those who have the necessary means for a, necessary means for a higher abide-ucation, or is it still possible to slack off manually? Does being a Great Dude require a pair of testicles, or can special ladies achieve the paramount peak of Dudeness as well?

We at the Church of the Latter-Day Dude often ponder such esoteric questions, especially after our sacramental Thai-stick shipment arrives each month. In our contemplations we get pretty close to discovering the mythical *El Duderado*, only to have the whole concept abate into a serious case of the munchies.

Truth is, when it comes to defining the elusive qualities of a Great Dude, it's often just, like, your opinion, man. You have your definition, I have mine. Even so, we can still get you a list of Dudes who exemplify takin' 'er easy in a world gone crazy...some of them *with* nail polish.

Of course, there have been plenty of Great Dudes across the sands of time, known and unknown, who have abided down through the ages but didn't make it to the finals in this

section. The ones we highlight here all come from various times and places, some have johnsons, some have beavers—but each has an unspoken message about abiding that we can take comfort in.

We sure hope you folks will dig their style.

Jesus and the Buddha: A Pair of Diggable Dudes

A philosopher by the name of Karl Jaspers, WFTO,[34] called these two Great Dudes paradigmatic individuals because

---

34 Wiser Feller Than Ourselves

they pretty much shaped the bulk of world civilization for centuries.

Now, "paradigmatic."

Do philosophers have to use so many cussed big words?

Instead of running around trying to show off how big our dictionaries are by using a word like "paradigmatic," let's just get down to cases. In our more laid-back parlance, we think Jesus and Buddha were a pair of diggable individuals who happened to change the world by taking it easy for all us uptight sinners.

Of Gods and Dudes

Millions of people around the world today worship Jesus and Siddhartha Gautama (the Buddha) as pure and perfect incarnations of something divine and otherworldly.

And that's cool.

There's no harm intended here to anyone's religious regimens, but the Editorial We at the Church of the Latter-Day Dude prefer to strip away all the halos and heavenly choruses surrounding Jesus and Siddhartha. When we do that, it's a whole lot easier to dig the human Dudes they were here on earth before they were posthumously promoted to upper cosmic management.

Spend just a few minutes browsing in the religion section of a bookstore, and you'll see there was no literal connection between these two earthbound guys.

- Jesus was born to a poor, teenage Jewish mother in a Middle Eastern backwater of the Roman Empire; 500 years earlier Siddhartha was a rich Hindu prince living the high life with his dad near the Himalayas.

- Jesus was employed as a carpenter under the rule of Roman fascists and uptight religious reactionaries; Siddhartha was sheltered in the palace of his times, partying with royal concubines on his dad's dime.
- Jesus was single (unless you're into the whole *Da Vinci Code* thing) and lived at home with his mom, brothers, and sisters; Siddhartha was married and had a little Gautamski on the way.

Yet, early in their lives they both dropped out of the unsatisfying roles their societies demanded they play and wandered off to find their own authentic way in the world: Jesus caught some rays out in the desert for a while, and Siddhartha chilled in the shade of a bodhi tree. By the time they rambled back to their respective square communities, Jesus and Siddhartha were all enlightened up and ready to spread their message of mellowing out to the masses.

Abiding Lessons

Despite the differences between Jesus and Siddhartha (poor vs. rich, working stiff vs. party guy, Messiah vs. Buddha), we can learn a lot from them when it comes to abiding.

While we're still working on the turning-water-into-wine thing (which we feel would really enhance our ability to take it easy), here are some proven, paradigmatic lessons about abiding that we can get from this pair of diggable Dudes:

Your ego is just the bagman, not the driver.

Jesus taught that if you really want to take it easy, you need to let go of your ego's steering wheel and let the cosmic GPS drive your fucking car, so to speak. Siddhartha went even further and said there never really was a steering wheel in the first place. Once you realize that, it's a lot easier to lay back and enjoy the ride.

Dig the eternal now, man.

What Jesus called the Kingdom of God wasn't a place we'll get to sometime in the future; it's already here all around us. We just need to slow down and take a look within ourselves. Wherever we are, it's down there somewhere. Siddhartha's Middle Path is the expressway to the heart of downtown Here-and-Now, a place most of us visit once in a while but where few of us actually live.

Stop worrying and go with the flow.

Most of us have workdays and tax brackets to deal with. Jesus liked to point out, however, that if birds and lilies don't worry about that shit, then why should we? There's something bigger than the phony reality of governments, corporations, and banks that's taking care of them...maybe it can take care of us, too, if we let it. Siddhartha said stressing out about life's illusions only leads to a world of pain where we call each other shithead and treat objects like women. And that's a real bummer, man.

Have good friends you can roll with.

After Jesus and Siddhartha tuned into their Dude selves, they didn't go all monastic on everyone. Like the Dude, they wandered through life getting along with just about everyone, from priests to prostitutes. On a personal level, though, they rolled with a posse of valued pals with whom they could kick back and break some bread, share some parables, start a new religion. The usual.

Lao-Tzu: It's Your Thing, Tao What You Wanna Do

There's a lot about Lao-Tzu we don't understand.

Like, how do you spell his name, for one thing: is it Lao-Tzu, Lao-Tse, Laozi, Lao Dan, Lao-baoski? Did he write the uncompromised draft of this thing called the *Tao Te Ching* by himself, or was it him and six other guys? Did Lao-Tzu even exist, or was he out of his element in what most of us call reality?

Well, dudes, we just don't know.

What we do know is that Lao-Tzu, whether real or myth, embodies the essence of Taoism, one of the most ancient expressions of what we call the Dude Way. Jesus and Siddhartha spent much of their lives blathering about the Dude Way in sermons and sutras to anyone who would listen, while centuries earlier Lao-Tzu captured the entire experience in a single phrase: "Fuck it" (loosely translated from Chinese).

That just about wraps it all up.

Originator of the Rebel Shrug

Legend has it that Lao-Tzu was a curator of the Royal Library in China sometime in the 6th century, before Jesus came along and reset the calendrical clocks on everyone.

One of the reasons we know so little about him (assuming he even existed) is that when he wasn't doing his day job re-stacking scrolls at the library, old Tzuder apparently liked to lie low in his bungalow doing his own thing. According to an account by a Chinaman named Ch'ien:

Lao-Tzu cultivated the Tao and its attributes,
the chief aim of his studies being how to keep himself
concealed and remain unknown.

Like the Dude, Lao-Tzu wasn't much interested in a life of ego-driven achievement. He knew from studying the Tao that living that stressed-out way was not in harmony with *The Way*: the natural, creative flow that really ties the universe together. All Lao-Tzu had to do was look around at the crumbling kingdom he was in to see what happens when you're not in tune with the Tao: fucking fascists throwing cups everywhere, nihilists threatening castration, people wondering where the money is.

Lao-Tzu didn't get all worked up about the world gone crazy he found himself in, though. That would have been very un-Tao. He didn't join a bunch of reactionaries waving Chinese tea bags around; he knew nihilism wasn't even an ethos and he didn't care where the bullshit money was because there never was any in the first place.

Instead, Lao-Tzu did nothing...nothing, except shrug and say: "Fuck it."

Scholars aren't sure whether he tattooed that on his forehead or not. But before heading out of town on his water buffalo with rust coloration, Lao-Tzu did jot down his answer for everything in a handful of short verses that became the *Tao Te Ching,* the Taoist holy book. Then he rode a-way out west somewhere between legend and myth, where he's abided ever since.

Abiding Lessons

As with Jesus and Siddhartha, some religious folks have made Lao-Tzu into a God. We think the philosophical Lao-baoski would have found that exhausting.

Here are a few uncomplicated things the down-to-earth Tzuder might have contemplated while doing some *tai chi* moves on his rug:

Do by not doing.

That is some kind of Eastern thing. Does a tumbleweed make itself tumble along or does it roll from a natural flow it can't control?

Keep things simple.

The beauty of Lao-Tzu's philosophy is its simplicity. Same goes with abiding through life. If things get too complex, something always goes wrong.

Nothing is real.

Not like Lennon said, but in the yin-yang sense that you can't have something without also having nothing, or have ups without downs, strikes without gutters.

Heraclitus and Epicurus: Life's All Fluxed Up, So Enjoy the Ups and Downs

The only frame of reference some folks have of "the Greeks" may involve restaurants that serve gyros (what's a "yee-ro"?), college fraternities and sororities, or those cheesy Hercules movies made in Italy back in the '60s.

Sure, people also think of all those guys with long beards roaming around ancient Greece blathering about the nature of reality, but the truth is, much of their philosophizing leaves a lot of us wondering what they fuck they were talking about.

Still, these two WFTOs were among the first to identify basic elements of the Dudeist ethos, and that's what earns them this lofty position in our pantheon of Great Dudes.

Heraclitus: Dude, Are You Fluxing This Up? Heraclitus was something of a crotchety Greek philosopher whose writings some folks considered cryptic and a bit stupefying.

We're not going to split hairs here, however. Regardless of what kind of guy he was, Heraclitus is revered by Dudeists for perceiving two fundamental tenets of abiding, if we understand them correctly:

- Everything in the universe is constantly in flux.
- There's a unity underlying opposites.

Heraclitus observed that, "you can never step into the same river twice." (Or, in the Lebowski lexicon, "You can never have your head dunked into the same bowl of toilet water twice, shithead.") Similarly, ups and downs, strikes and gutters...they're just different manifestations of that same ever-flowing reality.

He was basically pointing out that the essential nature of everything (rivers, toilet water, human beings, the cosmos) is one and always changing from moment to moment into something new and different. So you should just take it easy and go with that natural flow instead of getting all uptight trying to cling to a past that doesn't exist.

Epicurus: You Can't Worry About That Shit   Anyone who has an entire way of life named after him isn't exactly a lightweight.

As the founder of Epicureanism, Epicurus laid out a basic Dudeist philosophy that posits true happiness emerges from hanging out with friends, having a simple, self-sufficient lifestyle, and from learning to say "fuggedaboudit" when life is a bummer.

According to Epicurus, the goal of his philosophy was something he called "ataraxia," which is essentially Greek for "Just take it easy, *Manos*."

Although his name is ironically associated with high-end connoisseurship today, Epicurus was in fact a champion of thrift and simplicity. He may have even frowned upon indulging in physical pleasures like jerking off manually and might have minded if the Dude lit up a jay in his house. Nevertheless, the essential Epicurean approach to life was in harmony with Tony the Chauffeur's philosophy that the Dude dug so much:

"My wife's a pain in the ass. She's always busting my friggin' agates. My daughter's married to a jadrool loser bastard. And I got a rash so bad on my ass, I can't even sit down. But you know me. I can't complain."

Fuckin' A, man.

Abiding Lessons

Life continually goes on, man.

Consequently, one should make the most of it by going with the flow and sparking one up whenever possible. And step into the river from time to time, preferably with a cocktail and an inner tube.

Ups and downs, strikes and gutters…they're all the same.

The trick is to roll down the center between these extremes and abide.

Ataraxia…Fuggedaboudit…

Or as the Dude would say: "Life's too short, man. You can't worry about that shit."

Emily Dickinson: It's Your Roll, Dude

A common question we get here at the Church of the Latter-Day Dude (aside from "What the fuck are you talking about?") involves whether women can be Dudes. Not in Aerosmith's "Dude Looks Like a Lady" sense of the word, but in our preferred nomenclature.

The short answer? Shit yeah.

Being a "Dude" doesn't require having a johnson, man; it's all about shrugging off social conformity, tapping into something genuine, and abiding by its meaning. By that definition, Emily Dickinson out-Dudes most guys, which happens to make her a Great Dude in herstory.

Because I Could Not Stop for Dude

Considering her repressive Victorian New England time and place, Emily Dickinson was truly an original who went far beyond the female form of a poetic life to find a room all her own.

Unlike many of her poseur male contemporaries, Dickinson lived a completely uncompromised authentic life. While Walt Whitman is considered a Great Dude, the verse he unfolded was greeting-card doggerel compared to Dickinson's unique and innovative style. Although many women of her class at the time knew their domestic place and remained ostensibly demure, she spoke out unabashedly with a poetic voice that still reverberates in American literature.

Yeah, she was an antisocial eccentric. Yeah, she could be a tad Puritanical. Yeah, she remained pretty much obscure throughout her life. But none of these characteristics disqualified her from following the Dude Way.

While Dickinson refused to be treated like an object and hung out mostly by herself in her room at home, she cultivated a life devoid of pretense. She didn't indulge in bohemian doses of mind-altering substances, yet as an "inebriate of air" she got a buzz from simply being alive, man, as when she wrote:

> I taste a liquor never brewed—
> From Tankards scooped in Pearl—
> Not all the Vats upon the Rhine
> Yield such an Alcohol!

She also rejected the johnson-dominated religious metanarrative of her time, and chose instead to unfold her own living story rather than follow the Bible, a book that she called an "antique volume written by faded men."

Few people dug Dickinson's style while she was alive. After she went off to that big Folgers can in the sky, a self-appointed Editorial We took her jagged little poems and tried to smooth away their rough edges. Fucking fascists.

Yet regardless of what your gender identity may be, those of us who dig Emily Dickinson's style see her as a distinctly abiding Dude who went her own way and made writing poetry her very own zesty, natural enterprise.

Abiding Lessons

While some may think that it's a man's world, Dickinson showed that being a Dude is about more than having a pair of testicles. It has more to do with:

Having the courage to roll your own authentic way.

Dickinson shrugged off the stifling gender expectations of the Victorian era and tapped her true self. As anyone who has tried to shrug off the stifling gender expectations of our own time and place knows, that requires a lot of fortidude.

Valuing integrity and meaning in your life over fame and fortune.

Today a person's worth is often measured by the size of his or her bank account and level of celebrity. Abiding in the Dudely way, however, is more like Dickinson said: "I do not like the man who squanders life for fame; give me the man who living makes a name."

Getting high on being alive.

Contrary to some common misperceptions, being a Dude doesn't have to involve ingesting mind-altering elements. Dickinson's abiding example encourages us to "find ecstasy in life; the mere sense of living is joy enough." Far out. An addiction to being alive is a strict drug regimen we can dig.

Mark Twain: American Idle

"Dude" is a name Mark Twain probably would not have self-applied in his time and place.

Back then in the Wild West where Twain once abided, a "dude" really was some kind of eastern thing: someone from back East all gussied up in fancy clothes putting on western airs. A whiny rhinestone cowboy with a cleft asshole to boot.

Yeah, it was that bad.

Nevertheless, for us, Twain most definitely qualifies as a gen-u-wine Great Dude in history. In fact, he not only epitomizes the American Dudeist ethos—he dang near originated it.

A Pioneer in American Indolence

Long before hippies tuned in, dropped out, and flocked to San Francisco in the 1960s, Mark Twain turned his back on uptight Victorian society and lit out for the territory a-way out west in the 1860s. There, he tumbled around like a tumbling tumbleweed, living the life of a sagebrush bohemian: prospecting for gold he never found, hanging around with his eccentric pals, knocking back quite a few oat sodas. Keepin' it real.

And long before Jeff Spicoli, the Beach Boys' Dennis Wilson, or Donny Kerabatsos took to the waves, Twain was a surfer—maybe the first white guy, in fact, to surf the sunny beaches of Hawaii.

Looking back on his days hanging out with nude natives in the bosom of the Pacific, sunning himself under palm trees all day, Twain extolled the virtues of abiding in a place where "you are safe from the turmoil of life; you drowse your days away in a long deep dream of peace; the past is a forgotten thing, the present is heaven, the future you leave to take care of itself."

Far-out, man. Far fucking out.

Unlike a lot of hippies who traded in their tie-dyes and love beads for a beemer and a corner office, Twain always remained true to the spirit of languidness that helped make America the Land of the Free:

"I am no lazier now than I was 40 years ago," he observed late in life, "but that is because I reached the limit 40 years ago. You can't go beyond possibility."

Sure, Twain was not a hee-ro. Like most of us, he was torn throughout his life between his freewheelin' bum side and his ambitious drive to feed the monkey.

Nothing changes.

However, regardless of the strikes and gutters life rolled his way, Twain continued to abide. And in the stories he wrote that make us laugh to beat the band (especially the one about a slacker named Huck), he always reminds all of us sinners to just take it easy, man.

Abiding Lessons

Mark Twain remains an enduringly lazy icon of all things Dude.

Here are a few other lessons in Dudeliness you may not have learned about him while dozing off in English class.

Be cool racially.

Yeah, yeah, we know all about the whole "n-word" thing. But Mark Twain was actually pretty cool, racially. He criticized the reactionary police for harassing Asian immigrants in San Francisco; back East, he married into an abolitionist family, befriended Frederick Douglass, and paid for one of the first African Americans to attend Yale Law School.

If we can place his writings in that larger frame of reference, perhaps we won't get so uptight about some of the words he wrote. And if we don't get so hung up on his words, maybe we won't get so hung up with each other, no matter what our preferred nomenclatures may be.

Keep everything in perspective.

Most people are stressed out if they have a job, fear they might lose a job, or wish they could find a job. Employed or not, we run around chasing after money and spend much of our lives trying to achieve things that remain out of reach. We can't allow that negative energy to consume who we really are, though. As Twain observed:

> *In America, we hurry—which is well; but when the day's work is done, we go on thinking of losses and gains, we plan for the morrow, we even carry our business cares to bed with us...we burn up our energies with these excitements, and either die early or drop into a lean and mean old age...What a nation of*

thinkers we might be if we would only lay ourselves on the shelf occasionally and renew our edges!

Mark it, Dude. That is to say, Mark Twain it.

Don't forget to laugh to beat the band.

We're all sick of the bullshit pandemic plaguing the world today. Twain's remedy for it? A healthy dose of laughter. It's the only thing that blasts through all the B.S. and reminds us all that the cosmic joke is on us...so why not enjoy the punch line while you can.

Bob Marley: Rasta Far Out

Bob Marley has inspired millions of Trustafarians to get baked on college campuses and play hacky sack while skipping class. Highly revered by his Rastafarian compeers as a visionary prophet with one totally cool backbeat, his veneration for the sacred spliff also naturally qualifies him as an honorary high priest of our abiding ethos as well.

But when all the ganja smoke clears, it's plain to see that Marley's righteous jamming makes just about everyone want to come together and feel all right.

It's this positive musical vibe, combined with a life dedicated to takin' 'er easy, that, in our humble estimation, elevates Bob Marley to Great Dude status worldwide.

Lively Up Yourself

You'd think growing up poor in the rough reality of ghetto life in Jamaica would have caused Bob Marley to drag a lot of negative energy into life's tournament. Far from it. As he once put it in one of his reggae ruminations, he couldn't live that negative way but instead made way for a positive day.

That's not to say Marley stumbled in an herb-induced haze down the primrose path of positivity. We're not talking about Hannah Montana here.

His Third-World time and place was filled with deadly gang violence and warring political factions. Being bi-racial himself, Marley also had to deal with racially uptight whites and blacks. Yet, he always abided right down the middle of life's strikes and gutters, teaching folks how to take 'er easy in the First, Second, Third, and Fourth worlds of pain.

"Life is one big road with lots of signs," Marley preached in one Dudely discourse. "So when you riding through the ruts, don't complicate your mind. Flee from hate, mischief, and jealousy. Don't bury your thoughts, put your vision to reality. Wake up and live!"

Marley wasn't known for preachy pop-star platitudes, though. He put his positive vision into reality by helping to bring together the leaders of the two warring political parties in Jamaica during a concert. Even after being wounded beforehand by a bunch of gun-toting reactionaries, Marley abided right on through the concert to show that this aggression would not stand, man.

Marley's musical vibrations and positive groove weren't purely altruistic, of course. He was propelled to worldwide fame and made a ton of bones, or clams, or whatever you call it. Where some folks would get all hung up in the soul-numbing complications of such a rock 'n' roll lifestyle, he somehow remained plugged in to the creative abiding source of his Dude-like vibrations.

It's like Marley said: "The greatness of a man is not how much wealth he acquires, but in his integrity and his ability to affect those around him positively."

Although Bob Marley made it to the finals far too early, we can always take comfort in the fact that as he jams with Jah in the Life Everliving, this Great Dude's integrity and positivity will forever give anyone who wants to abide in his music a contact high.

Abiding Lessons

If you want a quick shortcut to takin' it easy, just kick back and dig a few Bob Marley tunes for a couple hours, with or without herbal assistance. You can also lively up yourself by contemplating some of this Rasta Dude's meditations.

Take time to see what condition your condition is in.

Like Marley asked: "Are you satisfied with the life you're living?" It's good to look under the hood often to check how full your satisfaction level is. If it's flat, stir it up.

Emancipate yourself from uptight thinking.

You're the only one, really, who can free yourself from the strands of stressed-out thought in your head.

"Money can't buy life."

A dying Bob Marley said these words to his son, Ziggy, but they are also cool words for the rest us to wake up and live by.

Georgia O'Keeffe and Diane di Prima: Strongly Vaginal Artists

As we pointed out in our section dude-icated to Emily Dickinson, the female form of being a Dude does not make us uncomfortable.

In fact, the Church of the Latter-Dude has ordained thousands of strongly vaginal Dudeist priests, founded a Virtual Shrine to Our Special Lady to promote the feminine aspects of our ethos, and we especially dig the style of the special ladies in our lives and those who regularly participate in our online communities.

Still, the Church can seem at times like a real sausage fest. That's why we admire these two female Dudes who held their own, so to speak, in zesty, creative enterprises that are often dominated by DRJs (dicks, rods, and johnsons).

Beaver Pictures

Georgia O'Keeffe may have denied that some of her paintings of flowers resembled the female form (parts, anyway), but there is no denying that a ground-breaking originality and intensely colorful beauty permeates all of her artwork.

While uber-modernist guys like Picasso were running around treating objects like women and trying to Bogart the art world, O'Keeffe did the Dudely thing and headed a-way out west to take it easy in a place called Taos, New Mexico. There, she painted vivid desert landscapes, immense blue skies, and sun-bleached animal bones that ended up revolutionizing modern art.

Yeah, O'Keeffe worked hard at her art (is working hard at something you love really work?). But she also recognized the importance of slowing down and finding the time to abide in the natural flow of things. She loved to lie on a bench beside a tree at night and gaze up through the branches at the stars.

"Nobody sees a flower really; it is so small," she once said, explaining her take-it-easy approach to creating art. "We haven't time, and to see takes time—like to have a friend takes time."

True that. Which is why we think O'Keeffe shows us that life doesn't imitate art; when you slow down and abide, life *becomes* art.

Writing Stories with Production Value...Feeling

Think about the 1950s Beat generation and most likely guys like Jack Kerouac, William Burroughs, and Allen Ginsburg will come be-bopping to mind. However, often overlooked among all these cool cats are their chilled-out female counterparts. The Beat Chicks, if you will.

These special lady friends, according to *Women of the Beat Generation*, "were compassionate, careless, charismatic, marching to a different drummer," all of which sounds pretty Dudely to us. So that's why poet, author, and teacher Diane di Prima, the "archetypal Beat woman," is in our gallery of Great Dudes.

In addition to writing volumes of poetry, di Prima raised feminist standards in adult entertainment with her erotic

Memoirs of a Beatnik. She also balanced a truly boho lifestyle with a disciplined life as a writer, thinker, publisher, and mother (who brought her five children along while taking it easy in ashrams and hanging out at Timothy Leary's trippy Millbrook community).

Thanks to special ladies like Diane di Prima, our understanding of what it means to be a Great Dude has come a long way, baby.

Abiding Lessons

Before women's lib and grrl power, these two Great Dudes abided in artistic and literary worlds dominated by rods, dicks, and johnsons and showed us that:

Taking it easy is gender-neutral.

Bowing out of the rat race, ignoring societal pressures, and living more simply and creatively are elements of a fulfilling *human* life, regardless of whether you have a pair of testicles.

Working hard at what you love is not a bummer.

O'Keeffe and di Prima didn't lounge around the pool all day painting their toenails green. Like many of the Great Dudes listed here, they worked hard not just to feed the monkey but to do things they truly dug.

Slowing down is how you find your path.

O'Keeffe regularly left the city for the slower, more natural pace of the desert; di Prima shrugged off the uptight gender roles and rat race of her time and abided in the bohemian slow lane. Had they been racing down life's highway singing

"Viva Las Vegas," they would've rushed right by and missed the Dudely sights on the road.

Wavy Gravy: Saint Misbehavin'

It may just be our opinion, man, but anyone who has had a flavor of Ben & Jerry's Ice Cream named after him has pretty much attained instant Great Dude status.

The late Grateful Dead guitarist Jerry Garcia, for instance, is memorialized by pint-sized monuments of munchie-crushing Cherry Garcia stocked in supermarket frozen dessert aisles. For a while there, the counter-culture clown and all-around decent human being called Wavy Gravy also had a nutty blend named after him.

Although Ben & Jerry's discontinued Gravy's ice cream brand a few years back, not even global warming can begin to melt away his cool, karmic legacy of compassionate craziness.

The Illegitimate Son of Harpo Marx and Mother Theresa[35]

"Wavy Gravy" isn't a name most of us would self-apply.

Although the actual handle Wavy Gravy's lovin' parents gave him was Hugh Romney, he never had much use for it. In 1969, when a comical misunderstanding led blues guitarist B.B. King to think Romney's name was Wavy Gravy, Romney felt that appellation fit right in there with his freaky self-actualization during the '60s.

---

35 That's how satirist Paul Krassner describes his friend Wavy Gravy.

When he was "Hugh Romney" in the early part of the decade, he had hung out in Greenwich Village with his pals Bob Dylan and Lenny Bruce, writing and performing poetry and rambling monologues. By the late '60s, though, "Wavy Gravy" seemed more appropriate for someone who found himself out west tripping with the Grateful Dead and founding a hippie commune on a hog farm.

Gravy also adopted his clownish persona around this time after getting roughed up and arrested by reactionary cops during antiwar protests. He started wearing clown make-up and clothes to demonstrations because, he figured, who wants to be seen beating up a clown?

It was at Woodstock, as real political reactionaries threatened to have the National Guard clear out the hippie haven, that Gravy's clownishness became deeply infused with the Dude Way.

During all the rain storms, bad acid, and a potential violent crackdown, he and the others running the concert nonetheless staved off the negative energy and conjured up three days of peace, love, and music. Gravy believes it was because they surrendered their individual egos to an amazing energy in the universe that worked through them to create a momentary muddy heaven on earth.

This energy continued to spill Wavy Gravy across the sands of time, inspiring him to use his clownish persona to make the world a better (and funnier) place.

As other '60s activists grew disillusioned and apathetic, Gravy helped feed starving refugees in Kathmandu, and he co-founded the Seva Foundation (which helps provide health to impoverished communities around the world). Today he regularly cheers up sick children in hospitals and he and his wife run a performing arts camp called Camp Winnarainbow for underprivileged kids (something like the Little Lebowski Urban Achievers, only a whole lot cooler).

We don't know about you, but in a world full of self-absorbed bozos, we take real comfort in Wavy Gravy's holy foolishness.

Mr. Gravy, forever may your freak flag wavy.

Abiding Lessons

With his lifelong dedication to improving the world through clownish activism, Wavy Gravy shows us there's more to abiding than lying around like a bunch of deadbeats.

Be a clown, be clown, be a clown.

Not the kind of clown that creeps out little kids, but the kindly jester/trickster/fool who pokes holes in our uptight, overly serious egos so that our deeper humanity can flow through.

Roll with the existential banana peels that slip you up.

Life can be really absurd sometimes, but getting all nihilistic about it won't help. The absurd's-eye-view doesn't make sense of it all, but it does help us roll through the whole durned human comedy with a smile on our faces. As Wavy Gravy put it: "Keep your sense of humor, my friend; if you don't have a sense of humor, it just isn't funny anymore."

Taking it easy also means taking care of basic human needs.

Slowing down and taking it easy helps you recognize the basic human needs that affect all of us, man. Why, if enough of us abide together and let the Dude Way work through us to meet those needs…we might just catch another glimpse of the heaven on earth that's already here all around us.

Jeff Bridges:
He's The Dude, Man…
That's What You Call Him

Some truths are so self-evident, they're hardly worth pointing out.

The bosom of the Pacific is really deep, for instance. The Himalayas, well, they're pretty big. The sun, as most physicists will attest, is very hot.

And Jeff Bridges, by our estimation, is one Great Dude.

A lot of folks identify Bridges with his iconic performance as the Dude in *The Big Lebowski*, but the character he played wasn't just the result of some kind of acting thing.

Far from it, dudes.

Sometimes There's a Man

By Jeff Bridges' own admission, there's a lot about the Dude that he would understand. Although the character is largely based on the Dude of History, Jeff Dowd, Bridges was a little freaked when he first read the script because he found the Dude to be so much like himself.

"I said, 'What is this?'" Bridges recalled in a PBS interview. "This is like nothing that I've ever done before. This is like—did you crash one of my high school parties?"

Bridges shares the Dude's counter-culture past, of course. Along with so many bright, flowering young men

GREAT DUDES
IN TV AND FILM HISTORY

Our Great Dude of Film, Jeffrey Lebowski, is only one of a long, laid-back line of fictional slackers lounging around in our pop culture imagination. Here's a brief sampling of some great TV and movie deadbeats that have made us laugh to beat the band.

Maynard G. Krebs, *The Many Loves of Dobie Gillis* The "G" stood for "Walter" (seriously, it was a silent "G"), but it could also stand for "Great Dude." This beloved beatnik bongo bopper, who grew faint at the mere mention of the word "work," is probably the first Dudeish character to take it easy in the white-bread world of early TV sitcoms.

Oddball, *Kelly's Heroes* Although not one to dabble in pacifism, this proto-hippie tank commander never let the negative energy of World War II or a bunch of fucking Nazis interfere with drinking some wine, eating some cheese, and catching some rays.

Easy Reader, *Electric Company* Never was learning to read so laid-back as when this Dude broke it down with: "Top to bottom, left to right. Reading stuff is outta sight!" Morgan Friedman played this recurring Hendrix-style hipster whose only goal in life was to read things and flirt with PBS chicks.

Dr. Johnny Fever and Venus Flytrap, *WKRP in Cincinnati* Thanks to this Dude-like DJ duo, the fictional citizens of Cincinnati could rock 'n' roll all day with Johnny Fever and mellow out overnight with Venus Flytrap's funky grooves. Perhaps the only radio station ever to have that whole musical yin-yang thing going on.

Rev. Jim Ignatowski, *Taxi* A spaced-out '60s sage who's more Dude than *the* Dude himself. Yeah, Jim could barely remember his name thanks to his more-than-just occasional acid flashbacks, but he could drive home deep truths that his fellow cabbies (and the rest of us) were too busy to pick up.

Ty Webb and Carl Spackler, *Caddyshack* Obviously, each of these Dudes was a golfer. Ty the rich guy taught us to be the ball and to just take it easy on and off the course; Carl the groundskeeper abided by avoiding work, eyeing the lady golfers, and combating his worthy fucking adversary, the Varmint Cong.

Jeff Spicoli, *Fast Times at Ridgemont High* What is it with the name "Jeff" and being a Dude? The patron saint of all things surfing, Spicoli summed up our ethos in this perfectly pithy riposte to another character's suggestion that he get a job: "What for? All I need are some tasty waves, a cool buzz, and I'm fine."

Ferris Bueller, *Ferris Bueller's Day Off* This righteous Dude quoted Lennon's "I am the Walrus" and believed in regularly taking it easy because, as he put it, "Life moves pretty fast. If you don't stop and look around once in a while, you could miss it."

Lloyd Dobler, *Say Anything* When he wasn't being a borderline stalker, Lloyd lived the intentional Dude life. In between kickboxing bouts, he took it easy with his buds and special lady friends, and espoused the Dudeist credo of refusing to "sell anything, buy anything, or process anything as a career."

For more on Great Dudes in History, please visit dudeism .com/greatdudes.

and women of his generation, he's smoked a lot of weed (although, ironically, he didn't toke while filming *Lebowski*), and he's probably had his fair share of acid flashbacks.

He and the Dude have other qualities in common, too, ranging from their self-effacing, down-to-earth manner to their ultra-casual clothing (the jellies and other pieces of clothing worn by the Dude came right out of Bridges' personal wardrobe).

Beyond these similarities, though, Bridges shares many important qualities with other Great Dudes in history we've included here. While being a self-confessed lazy man, Bridges is also one of the most steadily employed actors around, dude-icating himself to, and practicing, a craft he truly digs.

From his movie debut as an infant in 1951's *The Company She Keeps* to his performance as crotchety old Rooster Cogburn in the Coens' remake of *True Grit* (2010), Bridges has appeared in more than 60 film and TV productions across the sands of time, with his wide repertoire including comedies, dramas, mysteries, sci-fi, cartoons, documentary narration, and whatever-have-you. It seems that *Logjammin'*-style adult entertainment is the only kind of film he hasn't done.

Born into the Hollywood scene as he was (his mom, dad, and brother were all famous actors), you'd think Bridges would have ended up a kind of fragile, egomaniacal movie star with emotional problems. By all accounts, though, he's extremely cool to work with on the set and is generous and friendly with cast and crew alike.

Perhaps it's because he's into some kind of Eastern thing (specifically, Zen Buddhism) that Bridges apparently sees through the illusory nature of stardom and recognizes there's much more to life than waltzing around Tinseltown with a bunch of fucking strumpets. Unlike the Dude of Film, who wasn't much innerested in the whole matrimony/parenting thing, Bridges has also been married to his special lady, Susan, for more than 30 years and is a doting, loving dad to his three daughters.

Beyond acting and his cherished home life, Bridges is a purty good artist, musician, and photographer who devotes his time and talent to humanitarian causes like the End Hunger Network he founded in 1983.

In short, he's not only the Dude, he's one heckuva Great Dude, which puts him high in the running for Great Dude Worldwide. And because of that, we're, on a personal level, really enormous fans.

Abiding Lessons

Jeff Bridges has abided through quite a few cinematic strikes (like *Crazy Heart*) and gutters (*Heaven's Gate*), and rolled on through it all with an affable authenticity that proves nice guys can finish first.

Here are a few of his Dudely quotes to ponder while watching his film library:

Stay creative in all you do.

"When you start to engage with your creative processes, it shakes up all your impulses, and they all kind of inform one another."

When life's a bummer, look for the joy that's still down there somewhere.

"Sure, I get the blues. But what I try to do is apply joy to the blues, you know?"

Everything is everything and keeps on flowing on.

"This idea of how everything is interconnected, and the impermanence of things. It sums up the human condition to me, and it helps me on my path."

We're all in this together, man.

"Why can't we get together and make it a groovy trip for everyone?"

Why can't we, indeed?

THE BOOK OF REVOLUTIONS

Dudeist Prophecy

> The reason the world is so fucked up is
> we're undergoing evolution. And the reason
> our institutions, our traditional religions, are all
> crumbling, is because...they're no longer relevant.
> So it's time for us to create a new philosophy and
> perhaps even a new religion, you see. And that's
> okay 'cause that's our right, 'cause we are free
> children of God with minds who can imagine
> anything, and that's kind of our role.
> —*Bill Hicks*

There's a lot of blathering these days about the end of the world as we know it, but when hasn't there been?

It seems that folks in just about every generation believe they'll be the ones who make it to the finals of human history. Sometimes they think it will be something secular or nihilistic, like back in the late '90s when the Y2K bugaboo was going to cause civilization to collapse, or in the '50s and

'60s when one atomic bomb threatened to ruin your whole day forever.

When it comes to uptight thinking about the end of the world, though, secular apocalyptic theorists are a bunch of amateurs when compared to what various religions believe is going to happen. Most religions, being concerned with the big picture, try to give us a frame of reference for how this cosmic movie we've wandered into began (as in the *Book of Genesis*), and what's going to happen before the final credits

The Abide Guide

roll (such as what unfolds in the *Book of Revelations'* acid-flashback story).

Smarty-pants theologians even have an entire field of study dedicated to understanding the way a religion envisions how the sands of time will run out, something they call "eschatology." In the musty halls of theology departments, eschatology means the study of final things like death, the last judgment, humankind's ultimate destiny, and whatnot. There's also another level of meaning you get when you break the word down to its roots:

- The Latin phrase "e," meaning "out of," (as in *e pluribus, unum*), plus
- The guttural word "scat" (another word for "shit"), plus
- The suffix "-ology" ("the study of")

All of which gives you, if you squint your eyes just right: "The study of scaring the shit out of people."

That definition certainly applies to a lot of what's called prophecy, anyway.

For centuries, people around the world have loved to scare the shit out of each other with cryptic divinations about the End Times—from ancient Norse Pagans spooking themselves with the tale of *Ragnarok* (the cataclysmic final battle of the gods that would do to the universe what Jackie Treehorn's thugs did to the Dude's bungalow)—to the lucrative *Left Behind* franchise dramatizing what some Christians call the Rapture, with Kirk Cameron's performance in the series' film trilogy leaving many viewers wishing the world *would* end soon.

Of course, a religion's eschatology isn't always scary. On a metaphorical level in most apocalyptic stories, Good goes mano-a-mano with Evil. After Good prevails over its worthy fucking adversary, it creates a new, purified world where everyone (who survives) will kick back for all eternity.

Lots of people take comfort in that vision, which is one of the tasks that prophetic scripture hopes to achieve—that is, reassure believers that even when it looks as though the goddamn plane has hit the mountain, don't freak out, it's all going to be cool in the end...God or What-Have-You is in control, and as long as you're not rolling with a bunch of creeps and you don't contravene the holy by-laws, you'll be among those who win the tournament at the end of league play.

That take-it-easy metaphor is often overshadowed, however, by the scary literal connections people make between our time and place and apocalyptic texts. When reading prophetic writings, a lot of people don't focus the ultimately hopeful vision that this ancient literary genre offers. All some believers see is a bad moon on the rise and trouble on the way, to paraphrase a better singer than either of us.

Mayan Is Not the Preferred Nomenclature... Meso-American, Please

Consider all the fuss these days over the ancient Mayan calendar. There are a lot of folks who fear that because it ends in December 2012 the calendar suggests that some kind of cataclysmic, disaster-movie ending for the world is heading toward us. Not that you can blame them for seeing it that way. It seems that this thing we call Western civilization is collapsing from exhaustion all around us. With global warming, economic breakdown, wars, and social upheaval, it's easy to believe that humanity is increasingly out of its element.

So it sure is plausible to see the Mayan calendar as a cosmic alarm clock set to go off soon, letting everyone know that the party's over, oops, outta time, as Prince once sang.

Such a gloom-and-doom interpretation makes for a good blockbuster movie plot or a successful career in televangelism (where "prophet" is often confused with "profit"),[36] but it does little to help us abide. In fact, it does just the opposite.

A feller by the name of John Major Jenkins, however, has a more abiding take on what the Mayan calendar is really all about. Having studied Mayan religion a bit more in-depth than your average Hollywood screenwriter or profit-driven prophet, Jenkins asserts that the calendar isn't a doomsday clock at all. Instead, he believes its abrupt end in 2012 marks the beginning of a positive transformation in human consciousness.

There are a lot of ins and outs and eschatological strands to keep together in our heads with Jenkins' interpretation. Basically, though, he says that Mayan cosmology believes our sun will align with the heart of our galaxy during the winter solstice of 2012. Jenkins says the shamanic stargazers of

---

36 Whether he bases his prophecy on the Mayan calendar or not, Christian televangelist Jack Van Impe has suggested that 2012 will be an important year in terms of his interpretation of Biblical prophecy. But he also once claimed that UFOs are driven by satanic demons.

Mayan culture, who were amazingly advanced in their understanding of how the celestial sands of time flow, centered their entire calendar around this epochal event.

According to Mayan myth, the solar/galactic alignment does signify an ending, but it's the ending of an uptight age of selfishness in which human beings are woefully out of balance with ourselves, with each other, with nature, and with the universe (sound familiar?). In true yin-yang fashion, the calendar also marks the beginning...the initiation of a new, laid-back era, one in which humanity has a chance to reconnect with our Eternal Source—what we Dudeists call the Dude Way.[37]

If Jenkins' theory is true, who knows? Maybe 2012 won't be our final curtain call after all. Maybe it's the dawning of the Age of Abiding Us.

Our Revelation Is Not Over

Regardless of what prophetic frame of reference you have, we can't help but wonder whether prophecy even has a place in the Church of the Latter-Day Dude. After all, in the cinematic source of our worldview, *The Big Lebowski*:

- There really is no final confrontation between Good and Evil...We never even get to see the Dude and Walter bowl the Jesus and Liam in the play-offs.

---

37 For more information on John Major Jenkins' views, check out his website: alignment2012.com. Some folks, however, are skeptical about Jenkins' interpretation of the significance of 2012 in Mayan religion (www.2012hoax.org/john-major-jenkins). We're not advocating his views here, just saying that when it comes to prophecy, a lot of it is just, like, your opinion, man.

- No one is trying to scare the shit out of anyone. If anything, its laid-back folksiness hopes everyone will laugh to beat the band when they watch it.
- Nothing is wrapped up and no new era is promised. Life just goes on, man.

The Big Lebowski may not fit the traditional prophetic nomenclature, but we still believe it has an important prophetic function in Dudeism. Other religions have their prophetic stories, and we have ours. Only our story isn't all hung up on figuring out what happens in the End Times; we're all about remembering how to live the right way in These Here Times.

Believe it or not, that's what many religious prophets were really all about, too.

If we understand it correctly, these guys weren't running around telling everyone what dire things are going to happen in a few thousand years. Like Dudeist prophet Bill Hicks, they looked around and saw that their traditional religious and political institutions were no longer relevant to the real needs of their communities. Many prophets were actually trying to revive old forgotten truths about life among people living in new circumstances.

The Jewish prophet Isaiah reminded phony religious achievers that, to do what God really wants, they need to take care of society's marginalized bums. Jesus of Nazareth did his share of talking about the End Times, but he also had no idea when it would happen. Instead, he seemed more interested in kicking the rich fucks out of the temple, getting people to stop worrying so much, and encouraging everyone to be more like the lilies of the field (which aren't known for their exhausting lifestyle).

This kind of prophetic function isn't just limited to an ancient Jewish-Christian context. Buddha felt that more than 1,000 years of Hindu tradition and practice had become too complicated and was no longer releasing folks from their stressed-out suffering. He reminded everyone that enlightenment didn't involve a bunch of rituals, deprivation, or self-indulgence...it was really all about just sitting down and mindfully relaxing.

In politics too, people like Thomas Paine are credited with lighting up revolutions with their prophetic rhetoric. Paine saw prophets as inspired poets who were checking in to see what spiritual/political condition their community's condition was in. Following their lead in the political arena, he reminded oppressed subjects of out-of-touch monarchies that they are really free individuals capable of creating a new and more relevant world for themselves without the Royal We.

Even scientists can serve a prophetic function in reminding us who we really are in the grand scheme of things. When astronomer Carl Sagan saw a photo of Earth taken by the Voyager space probe from near Saturn, he reflected on how the smallness of this lonely speck, surrounded by the deep, vastness of space, "underscores our responsibility to deal more kindly with one another, and to preserve and cherish the pale blue dot, the only home we've ever known."

Like a true prophet, Sagan's view is far-out and down-to-earth all at the same time.

The Big Lebowski and the Three R's of Prophecy

The prophetic role, therefore, is an ongoing, evolutionary process that manifests itself in various ways...including in the form of a movie.

So in what way is our Sacred Source prophetic? Well, according to what we've laid out here, the prophetic role consists of these three R's: *Revelation* of a forgotten truth, *reminding* people of this forgotten truth, and *revolutionizing* their consciousness by making the forgotten truth relevant again.

- *Revelation*: In July 1998, the movie *Armageddon* was released. Its story about the impending doom of a giant asteroid hurtling toward Earth, combined with its allusion to the Biblical final battle between Good and Evil, tapped into the anxiety people felt about the looming new millennium. A few months before, *The Big Lebowski* had appeared, reassuring everyone that it was time to just take it easy, man. Life will go on. *Armageddon* was the year's top-grossing movie, while *The Big Lebowski* was considered a flop. Just goes to show how prophets are rarely popular when they first arrive on the scene.

- *Reminding*: Even though *The Big Lebowski* didn't fare well when it first came out, its eternal, laid-back ethos slowly began to resonate in an uptight, multitasking world, reminding people that abiding is really what life is all about.

- *Revolution*: It's been more than a decade since *The Big Lebowski* appeared. In that time, it has lit a worldwide relaxolution in consciousness that is redefining how we live according to abiding truths in These Here Times. It does this through annual Lebowski Fests, Dudeism's Day of the Dude celebrations on March 6, and by just kicking back and enjoying the proverbial ride.

After all, it is just a ride. That's what Bill Hicks called life: one big ride. And he prophesied that we can change the nature of that ride any time we want. We just need to loosen up our thinking, stop dragging around our negative energy, and trust that the universe isn't trying to scam anyone here.

I guess that's why we find Hicks so durn inneresting.

He could rant and rave like Walter, but he was basically pretty Dude-like in his outlook. He said, "Fuck it" to all the bullshit generated by those he condemned as "fevered egos that are tainting our collective unconscious and making us pay a higher psychic price than we imagine." Instead of scaring the shit out of us, he made us laugh our asses off. Ultimately, he called on us to find a little bit of heaven right here and now by creating a better ride for everyone, one where we all "explore space together, both inner and outer, forever, in peace."

That sounds a lot like Dudeism's answer for everything too. Why not join us for the ride?

The story may be ludicrous, but we can imagine where it goes from here together. If we will it, it is no dream.

DUDEIST MOVEMENTS

Dudeism Down Through the Ages

Just how old is Dudeism?

We here at the Church of the Latter-Day Dude have argued that it has existed in one form or another since before the dawn of human civilization.

Supporting our theory was a recent discovery of a huge stash of killer doobage found in the 2,700-year-old tomb of an ancient Caucasian shaman in what's now modern China. No less than three quarters of a kilo were found buried with the sorcerer, ostensibly to help keep him in a groovy frame of mind in the afterlife.

Of course, ancient dudes didn't have to die face down in the muck to make use of the blessed herbal enhancement. According to Greek historian Herodotus, Iranian nomads roamed around in the first millennium B.C., tossing bales of marijuana onto large bonfires, letting the clouds of smoke engulf them.

Talk about getting a contact high.

The Dudeist ethos, though, goes beyond lighting up a jay or breathing in smoke from a ganja bonfire. In contrast to the uptight and superficial life that society often demands we live, the Dude Way is really about living an authentic life that grows naturally from a laid-back sensibility.

We believe this sensibility, as part of the essential human spirit, has wafted across the sands of time in many different forms, sometimes prompted by THC consumption, but most often inspired by that inherent need people have to shrug off uptight thinking and just take it easy with each other.

One of the most recent manifestations of that need, of course, has been the growing cult around *The Big Lebowski*. Here are a few other literal connections we've made between historical movements and the ongoing relaxolution.

THE AXIAL AGE 800–200 BCE

Not to be confused with the "Axl Rose Age," in the 1980s, when there was a lamentable regression in human civilization, the Axial Age marked a dramatic shift forward in human consciousness around the world. During this time, lots of people decided to stop living in the fucking past and began to seek a new and vital spirituality grounded in the here and now.

Many fresh manifestations of the Dude Way emerged simultaneously around the world in the Axial Age. Lao-Tzu, Buddha, and the folks who wrote the Upanishads all contributed to creating some kind of Eastern thing in China and India; the prophet Isaiah was railing against the social injustice caused by rich fucks and real reactionaries in Palestine; and Heraclitus and other philosophers were pondering the nature of being and nothingness in ancient Greece.

Generations later, we're a bunch of religious deadbeats, still freeloading off the achievements of that transformative age. Ironically enough, what began as fluid new ways of understanding the cosmos and our place in it has mostly calcified into rigid, uptight sky-god thinking again.

Maybe it's time for a new Dudeist sequel to the Axial Age...*The Relaxial Age*? *The Axial Age II: Return of the Dude Way*?

SUFISM 7TH CENTURY CE–PRESENT

While it wasn't part of the Axial Age, Islam ushered in a new religious understanding of how best to make it to the finals. In the 7th century, the prophet Muhammad's revelation helped to unify various tribal groups across the sands of Arabia into one big round-robin.

Not exactly a lightweight.

However, not long after Muhammad's death in 632 CE, the fellers in Islam's league office got all wrapped up in worldly achievements and enforcing scriptural by-laws. Sufi dervishes came whirling along and reminded them that they can't worry about all that shit. Life's too short. Just take it easy and rest in the ecstasy of oneness with Allah.

One of the best known of these Sufi dudes was a Dude from Afghanistan by the name of Jalal ad-Muhammad Balkhi, who called himself "The Roman" (or, in the parlance of his times, Rumi). The zesty references he made in his poetry to laying around, drinking wine, and having coitus raised the ire of some Islamic reactionaries.

Even today, some uptight Muslims don't dig Rumi's (or the Sufis') style. But we, on a personal level, really take comfort in it.

TROUBADOURS 12TH–13TH CENTURIES

A long time before Creedence Clearwater Revival roamed the earth, traveling musician-poets toured parts of Europe performing new songs for the medieval masses. These proto-rock stars traveled from village to village and fed the monkey by entertaining common folks and nobility alike with their epic ballads about love, heroes, and other entertaining shtuff.

Playing their secularized songs before large crowds at fairs, weddings, and other celebrations (and singing in Middle English too, instead of Latin), these troubadudes brightened up the Dark Ages by spreading a festive, take-it-easy vibe and nudging medieval society away from a joyless feudal culture.

Some real reactionaries in the Church, along with the bubonic plague, stymied their movement for a while, but the troubadour revolution was far from over. As the prevalence of pop music over the past century attests, their Dudely beat goes on. Paying credence to this notion, one of the most important musical flashpoints of the '60s music revolution was called "The Troubadour."

ROMANTICISM 18TH–20TH CENTURIES

Compared to the Middle Ages' feudalism and superstitious religiosity, the Age of Enlightenment, industrialism, and the scientific revolution were good things. Parts anyway. The cold rationalism and social upheaval that also emerged from these movements, however, left a lot of folks' lives with no emotionally meaningful frame of reference.

From the end of the 18th century on through to the early 20th, the Romantic movement really tied Western culture together by investing it with story, production values... *feeling*.

As precursors to Maude Lebowski and Knox Harrington, these Romantic dudes redefined the visual arts as a means of personal expression; they established musical traditions that would ultimately result in the likes of Bob Dylan and Autobahn; they influenced revolutionary political movements that would inspire the Dude and six other guys to become the Seattle Seven; and as innovative literary narrators, they could tell a purty good story just like the Coens.

Yeah, Walter's sick Cynthia thing can also be found in Romanticism's overwrought emotionalism (just read Goethe's *The Sorrows of Young Werther*). But overall, the movement's legacy bestowed to Dudeism the precious gift of one of our most basic tenets: slowing down, savoring the here and now, and creatively following your heart.

Now, isn't that Romantic? Love, in the Dude sense of the word.

THE LUDDITES EARLY 18TH CENTURY

Once there was a group of folks who were inspired by a fictitious character to slow down and live more naturally human lives. No, we're not talking about Dudeism here, but a group that gets a bad rap these days, a group known as the Luddites.

Now, "Luddite." That's not a name most people would self-apply today, mainly because a Luddite is viewed as someone who doesn't share Jackie Treehorn's enthusiasm for technology. In fact, the word usually refers to technophobes who oppose (sometimes violently) industrial progress.

But that's just, like, high-tech modernity's opinion, man.

The word "Luddite" dates back to the early years of England's industrial revolution. Textile workers who rebelled against the mechanization of their times rallied around a working-class hero by the name of Ned Ludd. According to one legend, Ludd was whipped one day for idleness, so he took a hammer and smashed the hell out of some textile machines in retaliation.

Do you see what happens when you flog an idler with a lash?

Regardless of whether Ludd actually existed, textile workers whose way of life was threatened by industrialism followed his example and wrecked hundreds of weaving machines around England.

Their aggression may seem un-Dude, but the Luddites were resisting the industrialist impulse to have their humanity, in the parlance of Bob Dylan, turned into some machine. That's very Dudely indeed.

TRANSCENDENTALISM 19TH CENTURY

Transcendentalism is a big word for a movement that was really all about simplicity. Simplicity in religion (God is not apart from us; we are all *a part of* God); simplicity in living (living deliberately in the moment and in harmony with nature); and simplicity in...uh, losing your ego's train of thought.

A Unitarian minister and writer in Boston by the name of Ralph Waldo Emerson got the Transcendentalist ball rolling back in the 1830s as a middle way between the reactionary Calvinists and the intellectually uptight Unitarians. Because he thought both groups preached compulsively and without joy, Emerson left the ministry and hung out in Europe for a while with a bunch of his compeers in the Romantic movement. He was also one of the first Americans to get into some kind of Eastern thing after reading newly translated Hindu and Buddhist sacred texts.

Emerson wrapped up all these influences into one philosophy that urged everyone to stop waving dead theologies around and to abide in what he called the Oversoul, or the cosmic rug that really ties everyone and everything together.

In doing so, he helped to create a whole new American ethos that basically says: If you will it, dudes, it is no dream. A great deal of America's social reform can be said to have come to us directly from Emerson, down through the pages.

UTOPIANS 19TH CENTURY

Remember those heady days when people dropped out of square society to join counter-cultural communes and get back to the land, experiment with communism, and practice free love?

Yeah, the 1800s sure were pretty trippy times, weren't they?

That's when a number of "utopian" communities popped up around America. One of the most successful of these experiments in alternative living was the Oneida Colony in New York, where they practiced something called "Bible Communism." Everyone shared everything: the work (which included making silverware that Oneida Ltd. still produces today), the profits of their labor (no one had to go looking for a cash machine), and even each other (everyone helped everyone to conceive).

Not all utopian communities were into the whole free love thing (in fact, some were celibate), but they all did share with Oneida a deep sense of utopian idealism. That was cool until they started looking for some kind of perfectly idealized life removed from the world's messy complexities. As most of these Victorian hippies (and their modern compeers) learned, though, there is no perfectly idealized time and place. After all, "utopia" literally means "no place."

The Dude shows that no matter how messy and complex the world may be, you have to learn to just take it easy in the "now here." The search for a perfect utopia only leaves you nowhere.

And that's a bummer, man. That's a bummer. Because this is quite a pad we've got here.

HUMANISM 20TH CENTURY

Some folks would have you believe that all our troubles can be traced back to when Adam and his special lady friend Eve were evicted from their totally unspoiled pad in God's garden party. Consequently, humankind is fallen and needs to get back in good standing with the Big Guy.

Humanism, on the other hand, believes that human beings have evolved over the eons to a point where we have the capacity for self-realization and for taking care of each other right here and now without chopperin' in supernatural help.

Tracing their movement back to ancient philosophers like Socrates (who encouraged people to think for themselves) and Confucius (who thought it was possible to create a society that takes care of basic human needs), Humanists think humanity can develop its own meaningful frame of reference through science, the arts, and non-theistic spirituality.

They also believe the world provides us with all the natural resources we need to assist us on our journey of creative self-discovery. Scientist and great Humanist Carl Sagan, for example, found Dudely inspiration in firing up the nature-based content of a jay as he dug the billions and billions of whatnot out there in the cosmos and here on earth.[38]

For Humanists, then, we were never kicked out of the garden party. It's still going on here all around us. We just need to learn how to tend to it better together and abide in the plentiful bounty it can provide for everyone.

THE DIGGERS 1960s

Unlike the trendy hippie styles that became part of the mainstream in the '60s, this anarchist collective of artists, poets, and actors weren't hung up on making fashion statements. They were all about living as free men and women.

Appearing in San Francisco's Haight-Ashbury district in 1966, the Diggers took their name from a group of radical farmers who rejected money and private property in 17th-century England. The San Francisco Diggers revived the original Diggers' spirit in their time and place by rejecting a modern system ruled by "those who would kill us through dumb work, insane wars, [and a] dull money morality."

Unlike the Utopians, though, the Diggers didn't seclude themselves in serene, bucolic settings. They took their revolutionary, laid-back vibe directly to the streets of San Francisco and created new ways to provide free healthcare, free food, and free clothes to anyone who needed them. They also staged free community concerts, spontaneous street celebrations, and art happenings.

The Man couldn't absorb the potency of the Digger movement the way he did with the Beats and hippies, which

---

38 He even postulated in one of his books that the first agricultural crop may have been marijuana.

may be why the Diggers are largely forgotten today by official history. But with all the dumb work, insane wars, and dull money morality coming to light in our society today, perhaps the time is ripe for a new generation to dig the style of the Diggers once again.

SLOW MOVEMENT 1980s–PRESENT

There are many movements from the past 30 years or so that we could cite as examples of a call to live an overall Dude-like way.

Because we're into the whole brevity thing, though, it's easy enough to wrap them all up as compeers of something called the Slow Movement. It began in the '80s with a Dude by the name of Carlo Petrini, who led a campaign to stop a McDonalds from opening in Rome. It wasn't just Ronald McDonald he had a beef with, it was the entire in-and-out, fast-food culture that came along with the corporate clown.

Petrini's Slow Food movement was all about slowing down and taking time to prepare and savor local and organically grown food with your friends. Over the years, the movement has spread to all aspects of life, from work to parenting, from travel to fashion, from media to religion (such as Yours Dudely).

Far from being reactionary, the Slow Movement is all about reclaiming a more humane and satisfying quality of life that we've lost in our civilization's ever-increasing speed-of-sound pace. What's the good of progress and technology, after all, if we're all running around like a bunch of stressed-out assholes?

Back in the '60s, the hippie rallying cry was "Turn on, tune in, drop out." Today, the Slow Movement invites us all to "Slow down, chill out, enjoy life."

Or in our preferred nomenclature: "Abide."

CREATING A MORE DUDE-OCRATIC SOCIETY

The Politics of the Dude

The Big Lebowski fits within many cinematic genres. Broadly speaking, it's considered a comedy/crime/mystery, but it's also called a buddy movie, a *film noir* spoof of Raymond Chandler's *The Big Sleep*, a stoner flick, and it even has elements of Westerns, Busby Berkeley-style musicals, and porn.

But a political film? Now, that's not a genre most critics and fans where we come from would apply to *The Big Lebowski*. It's not because the movie lacks political references, though. With George H. W. Bush's assertion that Saddam Hussein's aggression would not stand, Walter's hawkish and libertarian rants about Vietnam and the First Amendment, and allusions to the Dude's past as a student radical in the '60s, the film offers a hodgepodge of American political sensibilities from the latter half of the 20th century.

It's because of this jumble of references, however, that this postmodern cult classic seems to have no coherent political frame of reference. Many overtly political films (like Frank Capra's *Mr. Smith Goes to Washington*) dramatize a clear political agenda. How can such a disjointed narrative as *The Big Lebowski* have a political point of view, with its stupefying array of nihilists, reactionaries, feminists, blathering burnouts, and volatile veterans rolling through the plot like tumbling tumbleweeds?

Although the film doesn't present an overt declaration, or manifesto, or whatever you call it, the boys down in the political science lab at the Church of the Latter-Day Dude

The Abide Guide

believe they have found some leads for an unspoken political message in *The Big Lebowski*. It's a message that might just help us as citizens in these fractious times form a more perfect union, establish justice, promote domestic tranquility, and protect our basic freedoms.

Well, at the very least, it will help us all just take it a little more easy these days. And that can be downright revolutionary in uptight times like these.

"The '90s Are the '60s Standing on Their Head" —Wavy Gravy

The Dude may not be what's typically seen as a hero, but as *The Big Lebowski's* main character, he most likely embodies the film's core politics, assuming it has any.

The only trouble is, at first glance, the Dude seems to have no lucid political philosophy...nothing beyond pacifism, anyway. In fact, on first impression, the Dude seems like little more than a befuddled burnout, an unemployed beach bum, an apathetic slacker.

Though there may be nothing inherently wrong with these traits, a viable political ethos they do not make.

Or do they?

To some, the Dude may be just a Venice Beach deadbeat that the square community doesn't give a shit about. To others, however, like the cowboy Stranger who introduces him to us, the Dude happens to be the man for his times. He fits right in there, apparently, and exemplifies something—a certain *dude sais quoi,* if you will—that uniquely epitomizes his moment.

But what is that something? How does it fit into his moment? In order to understand the Dude's politics, it's important to understand just what that something is. And to understand that, we have to understand the time and place he fit right into.

According to the Stranger, the story he unfolds for us takes place in Los Angeles around the time of our first conflict with Saddam and the Eye-rackies. It's possibly on or sometime after August 6, 1990, since that's when Bush made his statement about Saddam's aggression against Kuwait not standing. Aside from the war clouds gathering in the Persian Gulf at the time, America was politically and culturally adrift between two political eras: The Reagan/Bush '80s were limping to a close, while Clinton's decade, when the President would meet Monica Lewinsky and go looking for a cash machine, was yet to come.

During this fluxed-up period, there seemed to be a shift in the cultural winds as well, a change similar to what happened in the 1960s but with the potential to be even more systemically jolting.

In Seattle, for instance, Kurt Cobain[39] and Nirvana were about to deliver a grungy shock to stale corporate rock that would shake the music scene more fiercely than the lovable Beatles did. Emerging from a *psilocybin* mushroom cloud in the Southwest, a comedian dressed in black named Bill Hicks was savagely lambasting society's hypocrisies and pretentions

---

39 Innerestingly, Cobain's first band was a Creedence Clearwater Revival cover band.

with a devastating wit that probably would have left Lenny Bruce laughing to beat the band.

And in Los Angeles County, there was the mythical Dude in his bathrobe, sniffing a carton of creamer in the dairy aisle at Ralphs.

What do these personages from the early '90s have in common? Well, that's what we want to tell you about.

Give Me Liberty or...Hell, Lost My Train of Thought

The '60s, as a phenomenon, has become cliché and even something of a joke.

Beyond the classic rock that still has staying power today, when we think of the counter-culture of that era, images of stoned, goldbricking hippies dancing around in parks may come to mind, along with shaggy-haired radicals protesting in the streets and occupying college administration buildings.

That may have been what the millionaire Jeffrey Lebowski thought when he first saw the Dude, anyway. There, strolling casually and disheveled into his study was, for the Big Lebowski, the living embodiment of the '60s. As harmless and as unassuming as the Dude may seem to us, to a blustering Reaganite like the millionaire Lebowski what the Dude represented was no cliché and it was certainly no joke.

In his laid-back carelessness, El Duderino's appearance posed a real revolutionary threat to everything the Big Lebowski believed in (and benefitted from) since Reagan came to power in 1980. In the millionaire's glowering eyes, the Dude's long hair and uppity, something-for-nothing demands must have brought back memories of the '60s rebellion. That would account for the millionaire's hostility toward the Dude, and it explains why the old man starts yelling for no apparent reason that the Dude's "revolution" is over when the Dude was just talking about his rug.

Obviously, the bona fide revolution that rocked the world in the 1960s apparently still threatened the Big Lebowski. And with good reason—the Dude's generation shook the world back then. Many members of this generation (along with disaffected members of older generations) joined what's been called The Great Refusal. This movement, consisting of many loosely affiliated examples of social unrest, was basically a mass rejection of the stifling corporatist ethos of the 1950s. It wanted to eliminate that era's rigid race, class, and gender hierarchy; militarism; powerful corporations; mass marketing and consumerism; and a prevailing sense of depersonalization.

A new generation coming of age in the '60s rejected that grey-flannel conformity and envisioned a better society, one rooted in the more radical aspects of the American revolution heralded by the likes of Thomas Paine. "This was a period of unbridled optimism and enthusiasm among student activists," according to Martin Lee and Bruce Shlain's *Acid Dreams*. "The Cold War had finally thawed, and many were eager to flex their political muscle for a variety of issues: civil rights, disarmament, university reform, and so forth. Nothing less than a wholesale transformation of society was thought to be in the offing."

The rebellion, as Theodore Roszak points out in *The Making of Counter Culture*, emerged from two sometimes conflicting popular movements: the politically oriented New Left, which basically sought a broader, more direct form of democracy ("Power to the People"); and the social/cultural revolution of the Beats and the hippies, who were all about discovering personal meaning through individual liberation ("Do your own thing").

Despite such high aspirations and noble intentions, though, the '60s revolution lost its train of thought. As the decade wore on, political assassinations, factional in-fighting, violent reactionary backlash, that whole COINTEL-PRO thing, self-indulgence, and co-option by the square culture took a heavy toll on the movement's youthful idealism and energy. Nothing changes.

But for a moment there, with the free-speech movement, legislative triumphs of the civil rights movement, and other culture-transforming advances, the times, they did seem to be a-changin'. Far from shooting blanks, that generation was actually planting seeds: the seeds of modern feminism, sexual freedom, civil rights for all minorities, and the environmental movement. You could say that the '60s started a Slow Movement that's still going on.

And the Dude, well, he would have been right there at the heart of it all, drifting somewhere between New Left activism and Beat-hip bohemianism. In fact, it was the Dude who dang near got the revolution rolling, if we understand it correctly.

Student for a Dudeist Society

The mythical Dude of Film, Jeffrey Lebowski, is based on a very real Dude of History, a feller by the name of Jeff Dowd.[40]

Dowd, a movie producer friend of the Coen Brothers, served as the inspiration for the cinematic Dude in several ways: He has self-applied the name "Dude" since he was a kid; he digs bowling and imbibing White Russians; and he was the Seattle Seven...well, he and six other guys (actually, one of the Seven was a lady friend).

After an anti-Vietnam War protest they organized in Seattle turned violent, members of the Seattle Seven were arrested in 1970 and charged with conspiracy to incite a riot. The Seven belonged to a protest group at the University of Washington called the Seattle Liberation Front (SLF), which was affiliated with the radical anti-war Weather Underground faction. The Weathermen, as they also called themselves (after a Bob Dylan lyric), emerged after Students for a Democratic Society (SDS) disintegrated into chaos in 1969.

Before its collapse, SDS had galvanized what became known as the New Left in the early '60s with a manifesto called *The Port Huron Statement*. This document was for that decade's youth rebellion what Jefferson's *Declaration of Independence* or Thomas Paine's *Common Sense* was for the American revolution: a clarion call, only this one mobilized a generation to fight oppression and racism, end war, and make America a more humane, egalitarian society.

---

40 Notice how "Tao" and "Dude" combine to create his name. He is the Dowd.

Although Dowd had nothing to do with writing any draft of the Statement, compromised or otherwise, he was, like so many in his generation, profoundly inspired by it—hence his involvement with SDS and SLF. In many ways, Dowd's freewheeling activism and dedication to living a creative, self-determined life personifies what the Statement defined as the purpose of life: the "ancient, still unfulfilled conception of man attaining determining influence over his circumstances of life."

That's the literal connection between the Dude and the anarchic spirit of the '60s. It's also why we think it made the overachieving, millionaire Jeffrey Lebowski so uptight. As the sands of time were burying the Big Lebowski's beloved reactionary '80s, right there in his oppressively clean mansion sat the abiding, slovenly epitome of the '60s revolution wearing a wrinkled hoodie, T-shirt, and shorts.

And on a weekday, too.

Quest for the Dude's Uncompromised Port Huron Draft

As the mythical author of the uncompromised draft of *The Port Huron Statement*, the Dude represents the purest essence of the political values that shaped the '60s. In reality, though, a founding member of SDS named Tom Hayden was the one who wrote the bulk of the Statement. According to Hayden:

"In the movie *The Big Lebowski*, the aging, stoned hippie played by Jeff Bridges announces that he helped write the Port Huron Statement. We don't remember the 'Dude' being there..."

Now, Mr. Hayden, are we going to split hairs here?

Did Lao Tzu really pen the *Tao Te Ching*? Was there actually a historical Jesus who rolled from Nazareth? Was Bob Dylan the man in Robert Zimmerman or was it the other way around?

Well, dudes, we just don't know.

What we do know is that the Dude of Film was definitely there in spirit as Hayden and his SDS compeers pounded out their generation-defining statement in Port Huron. We've never been more certain of anything in our lives. Knowing that, is there a way to discern from the existing document what the Dude's first draft might have been had he actually written it? If so, are there any political lessons from the Dude's draft that are still relevant for us today?

To find an answer to these questions, we used something similar to the deconstructive methodology of the Jesus Seminar to identify fragments in Hayden's text that could have been from the Dude's lost, uncompromised first draft.[41]

Uncompromised Draft 1

In this version, we identified statements from Hayden's original document that reflect key aspects of what we know about the Dude's political views in *The Big Lebowski*.

---

41 The theologians and scholars on the Jesus Seminar attempt to separate what the historical Jesus actually said in the Gospels from what was added later by the Church.

The Dude was opposed to treating objects like women.

Hayden's Version: *We oppose the depersonalization that reduces human beings to the status of things.*

While the Dude dismisses the millionaire Lebowski's overinflated sense of power, he draws from a deeper, more compassionate, and more authentic source of power.

Hayden's Version: *We would replace power rooted in possession, privilege, or circumstance by power and uniqueness rooted in love, reflectiveness, reason, and creativity.*

The Dude was a pacifist.

Hayden's Version: *In social change or interchange, we find violence to be abhorrent because it requires generally the transformation of the target, be it a human being or a community of people, into a depersonalized object of hate.*

The Dude was his own person, as unimpressed by the self-importance of others as he was unconcerned about what others thought of him.

Hayden's Version: *The goal of humanity and society should be human independence: a concern not with image of popularity but with finding a meaning in life that is personally authentic… This kind of independence does not mean egotistic individualism— the object is not to have one's way so much as it is to have a way that is one's own.*

These inspiring words reflect values that a young, idealistic, pre-Thai stick Dude could very well have written had he existed. But that's just, like, our opinion, man. While the sensibilities expressed are certainly Dudeist in spirit, we admit they seem a bit wordy and rambling for someone like the Dude, pre- or post-Thai stick inhalation.

So cutting from the document anything that seemed too verbose for someone who uses as few non-cuss words as the Dude does, we came up with the following essential version, also found in Hayden's original.

Uncompromised Draft 2

We need not indulge in illusions.

That sentence just about wraps it all up, doesn't it?

It's easy to imagine a young Dude back in '61 scribbling it down, tossing it to his more ideologically driven compeers, and cruising over to the Port Huron bowling alley to roll a few frames and enjoy a pitcher of cheap beer.

In the midst of a burgeoning revolution, we imagine the Dude would have said, paraphrasing words attributed to Emma Goldman: "If I can't abide, I don't want to be in your revolution, man."

A Duder World Is Possible

As we pointed out in the beginning, we do live in uptight times that test our laid-back souls, do we not?

War. Poverty. Natural disasters. Economic crisis.

There hasn't been a coherent revolutionary movement hoping to tackle these issues since the '60s. That heady potential for a new revolution in the early '90s? Well, it seemed to die with Cobain and Hicks and pretty much vanished altogether with the tragic appearance of the Backstreet Boys in the mid-'90s.

And what about the Dude? Didn't he basically abandon his youthful idealism after the '60s became, like everything else, a wholly owned subsidiary of Corporate America? How else do you explain his move from SDS radical to Metallica roadie to unemployed bum?

It's enough to make you think the millionaire Lebowski was right: Maybe the bums did lose. But that's just the stressful times talking. No need for condolences just yet.

What happened during the '60s and early '90s wasn't just confined to those times and places. The spirit of the Dude Way that emerged then abides throughout time, sometimes going underground, sometimes directly shaking the foundations, but always keeping the whole human comedy perpetuating itself down through the generations in freedom, peace, and community.

It's there in our basic human need to relax as members of inclusive communities where everyone is free to share some burgers, some beers, a few laughs, and whatnot.

It's there in our fragile yearning for peace and our need to do the right thing as a person, a community, and a nation, whatever the cost.

It's there in the vision of a free, cooperative society that Tom Hayden and Jeff Dowd struggled for, where it's not as important to get one's way as it is to create a truly meaningful way that is one's own.

That's what the Dude did, even when he was working as a roadie for a bunch of assholes. He always followed a personally meaningful path that was his own. He rejected the radical extremism of the New Left as much as he rejected the grey-flannel conformity it sought to liberate, and abided instead in the Dude Way.

What does that mean? Simply put, amid life's strikes and gutters, through all his bowling, driving around, and occasional acid flashbacking, the Dude always trusted his own perceptions and ideas and preferences instead of cleaving to some second-draft dogma about the way things should be. In a world where political and economic systems that are theoretically supposed to serve humanity's needs end up controlling, exploiting, and even crushing our individuality and integrity, that's a revolutionary act.

When we abide in our personal Dude Way and then groove together in the larger, universal Dude Way, we ensure that our eternal revolution is far from over. The reason we are able to take comfort in this is that so many Great Dudes have abided in the same way before us.

Now it's your roll.

A Duder world is possible. The revolution is not over. It just lost its train of thought there.

CINEMA VERTE
Stoner Films and The Big Lebowski

Many people place *The Big Lebowski* high in the running as a classic stoner movie. Sure, some purist fans of this genre debate whether the film really fits in this category, but our stoner friends are prone to debate just about anything after lighting up a bowl.

Regardless of which side you're on, though, at the heart of the debate is a worthy fucking question: What makes a stoner movie? Is it about doing a doobie, whatever the cost? Or, because these films are mostly about male bonding, does it have something to do with what makes a bud, man? On a more philosophical level: Are these movies only about hedonistic self-indulgence or, once the purplish haze clears, is there something more far-out going on?

These are the burning issues we'll try to spark up in this limber-minded section.

What Makes a Stoner Movie?

It seems easy enough to define this kind of film, doesn't it? Obviously, it's a movie where characters get stoned on cannabis, hence the "stoner" prefix. Others posit an even broader definition: It's any movie considered especially enjoyable when you're high.

It's a much more complicated case than that, though. There are plenty of movies with a lot of pot smoking that don't quite make it to the stoner finals (*Platoon*, for instance). Likewise, people can enjoy just about any flick while partaking of the herb, while, on the other hand, lots of people who never toke up at all can appreciate a good stoner movie.

Although there are wide-ranging variations within any film genre, there are also some key characteristics that classify a movie within a given category. While *cinema verite* (French for "truthy cinema") encompasses many different kinds of movies, for example, they all have a stripped down, documentary style to them. The stoner film genre (or, to coin a phrase, *cinema verte*..."cinema green" in English) also consists of a variety of films that all share some basic elements.

To begin with, the "green" in *cinema verte* is, of course, the green herb itself. As the main ingredient, it blatantly colors everything about the plot of a film. This trait, in fact, is why some contend that *The Big Lebowski* isn't really a stoner movie. Yes, the Dude gets high, but does his usage play a central part in the movie's narrative? We'll stash this question away for later.

For now, let's look at the other common themes of *cinema verte*:

- Friendship (especially between two close buds)
- Casual sex (or the frustrated desire to get laid)

- Low-brow humor (often featuring body parts and functions)
- Violence (typically played for laughs, but sometimes not)
- Uptight authority figures (parents, police, bosses), nerdy or snooty compeers
- A convoluted adventure/crazy party climax/whatnot

A Stoner Movie
Frame of Reference

With all the high jinks going on in stoner films, it's easy to assume that *cinema verte* is merely escapist entertainment with nothing more significant to say about life than "Everybody must get stoned." Beyond all the bong hits and potty humor, though, there is an underlying philosophy that ties all the thematic strands listed above together into a bona fide frame of reference.

In general, the stoner movie worldview is an absurdist one. It rejects and ridicules the so-called serious values of uptight society (careerism, social climbing, etc.) as phony and unfulfilling. Smoking pot helps the main characters in stoner movies keep it real in a screwed-up world dominated by these values. Main characters are also typically marginalized by the uptight world because of their race or lower-class status, or because they feel alienated from their middle-class background. Most are unemployed or wasting their lives in dead-end jobs.

The absurdist ethos of *cinema verte* isn't surprising, considering how it's fueled by something called "wacky tobacky." There is also, however, a sharp, subversive element to stoner movies. Whether you agree with it or not, the contention that pot opens your mind is a major subtext of the stoner movie philosophy. Social satirist Bill Hicks expressed the tenets of this view when he observed that:

- Smoking pot doesn't de-motivate you, it helps you realize that some things just aren't worth the fucking effort.

- Naturally grown substances that liberate your mind (like pot) are against the law, while mind-numbing, corporate-produced drugs like alcohol are legal.

It may be the seditious power of "marihuana," in fact, that has been freaking out the power structure since at least the 1930s. What other reason could there be (aside from the titillating shock value) for over-the-top propaganda films like *Reefer Madness* and *Devil's Harvest* from the '30s and '40s? In these hysterical histrionics, one puff of demon weed instantly turns clean-cut white folks into homicidal sex maniacs.

The scare tactics of these paraquat productions influenced the way mainstream movies portrayed grass...until *Easy Rider* roared onto the national scene in 1969, that is. Although dated in some parts now, in its day this proto-stoner film was considered quite revolutionary (cinematically and politically).

The plot involves two hippie buddies (Peter Fonda and Dennis Hopper) who score big on a drug deal and head out on their choppers across America. In the course of their journey, we learn some cool things (that the word "dude," according to Fonda's character, means "nice guy, a regular sort of person"), and some uncool things (that the personal freedom Fonda and Hopper enjoy through copious pot use threatens the up-tight world).

That last point in particular seems to be the movie's main theme. As Jack Nicholson's character says: "It's real hard to be free when you are bought and sold in the market-place...Oh, yeah, they're gonna talk to you, and talk to you, and talk to you about individual freedom. But if they see a free individual, it's gonna scare 'em."

Fonda's and Hopper's freedom, as it turns out, is one toke over the line in an uptight society, which ends up getting them blown away by a couple of reactionaries with a shotgun.

It was a bummer, man.

But then, a decade later, all that negative energy would burn out and go...*Up in Smoke*.

The Grandfather (or Big Bambuski) of Stoner Films

By the time Cheech and Chong released *Up in Smoke* in 1978, the comedy duo had already blazed a long trail in the reefer fields of drug-related humor. Compared favorably to classic comedy teams like Crosby and Hope or Abbott and Costello, Cheech and Chong defined humor in the '70s with inventive live performances and a string of hit albums.

The marijuana-laced comedy of *Up in Smoke* also established the standard formula of *cinema verte* movies already discussed:

- A friendship between two marginalized characters (Pedro and Man) coasting through an absurdly random world
- Humor about casual sex and body functions
- Mild violence (Pedro's cousin has a Vietnam flashback)
- Uptight authority figures (mainly law enforcement)
- A climactic music competition that Pedro and Man win because their van, made out of something called

"fiberweed," catches on fire and the smoke gets everyone zonked

- Unrepentant pot use while mocking square values (a
judge attempts to pass off a pitcher of vodka as water
during Pedro and Man's drug trial)

Despite bombing with critics when it first appeared (and
even today it has an abysmal rating on rottentomatoes.com),
Up in Smoke remains one of the most popular movies ever
made, raking in $41,590,893 in 1978 and over $28 million in
rental sales in the years since.

The Big Lebowski:
Stoner Flick or Not?

It should be pretty clear that *The Big Lebowski*, which came
out in 1998 as the stoner movie genre was beginning to boom
(see "Growing Like a Weed," page 150), has all the standard
elements of *cinema verte* mentioned here: buddy bonding,
casual sex, violence, uptight reactionaries, and a freewheeling misadventure toward solving a convoluted mystery. Joel
and Ethan Coen even seem to pay homage to *Up in Smoke*
in the scene where the Dude flicks a joint onto his lap while
driving around and drinking a beer. At the end of *Up in Smoke,*
Cheech also loses a joint in his lap while driving, and Chong
responds by dousing his friend's crotch with beer.

Still, there are some fans of *cinema verte* who don't
include *The Big Lebowski* as part of the genre, mainly because
the Dude only smokes herb briefly on-screen four times:
once while with the millionaire Lebowski, once in the tub,

GROWING LIKE A WEED:
THE PROLIFERATION OF STONER FILMS

Despite the success of *Up in Smoke*, it would take more than a decade for *cinema verte* to fully blossom into a genre of its own. Yeah, there were plenty of movies featuring ample pot use before and after Cheech and Chong's film was released. It took *Up in Smoke*, though, to infuse the dour stoner template established by *Easy Rider* with a potent hit of comedy.

With the success of Richard Linklater's stoner classic *Dazed and Confused* in 1993, the category began to grow faster than a hybrid of cannabis and kudzu. *Dazed and Confused* and most of the stoner movies that followed adhere to the basic formula established by *Easy Rider* and *Up in Smoke*. Here is a list of notable variations from the past twenty years that regularly show up on lists of top stoner films.

Dazed and Confused (1993)   Set on the last day of school in 1976, this film has a Great Dude in Film (Ron Slater) but also qualifies as a Dudeist cautionary tale about how takin' it easy can go awry. While it has all the elements of a stoner movie, the movie's ambiguous ending can leave you wondering if the main character (Randall "Pink" Floyd) wasn't dazed and confused in making a choice that may shape his life for years to come.

Friday (1995)   This first African-American stoner comedy, set in downtown Los Angeles, follows the antics of recently unemployed Craig Jones (played by Ice Cube) and his stoner friend, Smokey. "I know you don't smoke weed," Smokey consoles Craig, "but I'm gonna get you high today, 'cause it's Friday, you ain't got no job...and you ain't got shit to do."

Half-Baked (1998)   Although Dave Chappelle's breakthrough flick kind of sells out in the end when his character swears off pot (a breach of the *cinema verte* code), the cross section of pothead celebrities who make cameos, ranging from Snoop Dogg to Willie Nelson, really ties the stoner ethos together. The movie even contributed a new euphemism to the pothead lexicon: "I wanna talk to Sampson."

Harold and Kumar Go to White Castle (2004)   A true classic in *cinema verte*, this flick follows the epic quest Harold and Kumar embark upon to find an elusive White Castle restaurant after getting blazed one night. No matter how odd their odyssey becomes (such as riding a stoned cheetah and picking up a hitchhiker who turns out to be a hopped-up Neil Patrick Harris), the duo learns that the universe tends to unfold as it should.

Smiley Face (2007)   Anna Faris has the distinction of being *cinema verte*'s first female stoner in a lead role. She plays Jane, an economics major back in college, who is now an unemployed, bong-smoking actor. Although her misadventures showcase many classic stoner movie elements, the basically friendless Jane is one of the few characters in the genre who gets busted and punished in the end.

Pineapple Express (2008)   According to the movie's prologue, past secret military experiments on a smokable substance called "Item 9" resulted in disrespect for authority and an insatiable desire for be-bop and boobies. Likewise, a modern-day blend of pot called "pineapple express" sparks a lot of hilarious social disorder that unfortunately devolves into an outlandish level of violence by the movie's end.

once while driving, and once post-coitus with Maude. Aside from contributing to the collision with a dumpster, pot, and instances where the Dude tokes up, seem rather incidental to the overall story. Because pot defines just about every aspect of a stoner film plot, it may be tough to say whether it has a strong enough influence on the Coen Brothers' classic to qualify it as a genuine stoner movie.

Our Dude-like answer: Does the pope shit in the woods?

The Big Lebowski not only ranks high in the running of classic stoner movies, it also transcends the *cinema verte* genre as well. Despite rarely lighting up on screen, the Dude, it's important to remember, is pretty stoned through most of the film.

That isn't the idle speculation of people who have too much time on their hands to think about shit like this. According to Jeff Bridges, the Dude burned many more jays within the movie's timeframe than we actually see. Before filming a scene, in fact, Bridges would ask the Coen Brothers whether the Dude would have smoked a joint on his way to where the scene takes place. Because the Coens said he probably would have, Bridges essentially played the Dude as baked in most scenes.

Because most of the movie unfolds from the Dude's point of view, the film's narrative is almost entirely influenced by his use of marijuana. That would explain many of *The Big Lebowski's* more baffling aspects, such as the various tangled strands of plot that don't really go anywhere, the muddled references and confused sense of time (is it August 1990, when Bush made his comment about Saddam's aggression, or is it September 1991, as the Dude writes on his check?), and even the odd and possibly hallucinated appearances of the Stranger.

Abiding in a Universe That Tends to Unfold as It Should

So, *The Big Lebowski* really does fit right in there with the absurdist *cinema verte* worldview. However, as with other Coen Brothers' films, it also transcends the genre.

This is often how the Coens work: While remaining true to a common movie type, they infuse it with larger and deeper philosophical undercurrents that transform a familiar standard into something new and unexpectedly profound. Think of *The Hudsucker Proxy*—the Coens give the standard screwball comedy formula a new level of depth by adding notions of karma and other elements of Eastern philosophy to it.

The same is true of stoner films and *The Big Lebowski*.

In addition to sharing a generally absurdist worldview, most of the movies in the *cinema verte* genre have their own philosophical take on making sense of life in a random and, at times, seemingly meaningless universe. For films like *Up in Smoke,* it is hedonism. Beyond the "party hearty" ethos, many stoner films also try to impart on some level a kind of life lesson. The subtext in *Friday*, for example, focuses on what it really means to be a man in the 'hood.

Few *cinema verte* movies, however, offer what would be considered a spiritual or religious insight into life (which is odd, considering that many people around the world revere ganja as a sacrament). One outstanding exception is *Harold and Kumar Go to White Castle*. No matter how crazy and outrageous life gets for our pothead protagonists, *Harold and Kumar* reassures us that the universe ultimately tends to unfold as it should. If we roll with it, everything most likely will work out. As reassuring as this moral is, though, it seems peripheral to the film's overriding fixation on scoring weed, eating hamburgers, and getting laid.

That's why we believe *The Big Lebowski* is the cultural phenomenon it is today. It takes the popular and somewhat superficial, lighthearted stoner formula and uses it to tap deep life currents. True to form, the Coens remain faithful to the genre's standard formula (especially the subversive emphasis on personal freedom), but de-emphasize all the pot and sex while introducing much deeper philosophical elements: Eastern philosophy, feminism, radical politics (on the left and right), class tensions, even a poignant glimpse into mortality at Donny's funeral.

Joel and Ethan raise the stoner film to the level of epic art. As with most great works of human imagination, *The Big Lebowski* asks its audience big questions rather than offering pat answers. Most other stoner movies tend to preach an easy answer to everything that usually involves simply burning a blunt.

At the heart of *The Big Lebowski*, though, there is no easy answer for anything in life, least of all one to be found by getting high. The Dude's stoned reveries, in fact, are usually rudely disrupted by nihilists threatening castration or by driving his car into a dumpster. That's probably why we find the movie so enduringly inneresting. It resonates, so to speak, with many of the challenges and ambiguities clouding our own lives.

As we listen to the Dude's convoluted story, we also see that everything in his world is disjointed. Words have no common meaning. Situations are arbitrary and chaotic. No one's identity is clear or certain. After watching the movie for the first time, we feel like clueless children who wandered into the middle of something we don't entirely understand. We may even get the uneasy sense when the movie's over that we've wandered into the middle of our own lives with no firm idea of what's really going on.

Rather than feeling nihilistic despair, though, we take comfort in how, through all of life's ups and downs and existential absurdities, the Dude abides. And if someone like him can, perhaps so will we, with or without lighting up a jay. If we just relax and allow it to, well, the universe will tend to unfold as it should. In other words, it's a trip.

And that's a highly valued insight, is it not?

SUBJECTS LIKE WOMEN
Dudeist Feminism

Sometimes people get the wrong idea that Dudeism is a Brotherhood Shamus, with no sisters allowed. Far from it, dude. Though Dudeism's followers are mostly good men and thurrah, we've got a whole lot of special ladies in our ranks. While we can dig a nondairy version of our holy cocktail, like the Dude, ultimately we prefer half-and-half.

Perhaps it all comes down to the word "Dudeism." Now, "Dude," that's not a name most women would self-apply where we come from. But that's only because they aren't privy to the new gist. What makes a Dude? The way we see it, "dude" describes what's in your mind, not your pants.

Of course, the word "dude" has changed dramatically in meaning since it first arrived on the U.S. East Coast from England, and made its way westward with the wagons until it reached the bosom of the Pacific Ocean.

It evolved from describing a fastidious and romantically minded intellectual fellow to describing a privileged fron-tiersman, to an urban black alpha-male, to a languid beatnik poet until finally becoming a term of respect cleansed of all

its elite connotations by 1960s and 1970s hippie and surfer culture.[42] "Dude" is also increasingly losing its gender affiliation, though the transformation isn't yet complete. While some lady friends aren't into the whole "dude-ity" thing, it's not uncommon for a growing number of women (especially in California) to self-apply the handle "dude" the same way we refer to a group of people as "you guys" regardless of whether they're sporting pairs of testicles or not.

In addition to getting everyone, male and female, to just take it easy, one of Dudeism's objectives is to rid the word "dude" of any masculine bias. Dudeists aren't hung up on

42 Dude Defined: http://bit.ly/bJnIqe.

issues of masculinity or femininity. The vagina, man, is not the issue here.

Yeah, gender-free nomenclature can cause misunderstanding, of course. But all Western languages, reflecting a patriarchal ethos, are compromised by a "no-women-clature" gender bias: from the obvious "man" and "mankind" ("Sometimes there's a man...") to the habit of referring to unnamed individuals as "he" ("Every bum's lot in life is his own responsibility regardless of whom he chooses to blame"). As Walter puts it, "We've got a language problem here." Dudeism wants to help resolve it by co-opting the word "dude" and promoting it to suit our own special-innerest group. After all, people did the same thing with "gay," right?

Now aside from etymology, there might be other reasons why we have a-ways to go when it comes to making Dudeism as appealing to women as it is to men. We suspect that a big part of the problem comes from societal norms and expectations that tell women that, in short, they shouldn't take it easy. Now that's fucking interesting. And it's also a bummer man, it's a bummer.

The average women's magazine might sport the occasional novel review or bit of politics, but they're almost entirely catalogs of beauty tips, weight-loss schemes, and sexual tricks to please your male partner. Movie heroines generally play second fiddle to the intellectual or muscular male lead; they're either whining victims of male mistreatment, or they're man-obsessed and fashion-crazed *Sex and the City* wannabes. While most popular female role models are nubile young pop stars more admired for their abs than abilities (their glory is ludicrous!), truly admirable and powerful women like Oprah or Hillary Clinton are often judged more on their appearance than intellectual acumen. Forget about the fucking cameltoe!

Does the female form (the original, uncosmeticized first draft) make people uncomfortable? Fucking flesh fascists. We're sympathizing here, dudes. Our society treats women like subjects, man, and as a result, when it comes to giving birth to their authentic selves, it does not properly help them to conceive.

To help us get down to cases, we've invited a group of prominent female Dudeists to take part in this a-here round-robin—a series of questions about *The Big Lebowski*, Dudeism, and Special Ladyism. Affectionately referred to as "The Maude Squad," they are the women for their time and place. They really help tie our quorum together. They are:

- **Rev. Stella Quinn**, High Priest of Zymurgy, Contributor to the *Dudespaper*, and technological advisor.
- **Rev. Mother Duderior** (a.k.a. Tracy Glover, a.k.a. Matti Sim) Active member of the clergy, the *Dudespaper*'s Scottish correspondent.
- **Rev. Andrea Maria Atenas** One of the founding Dudes of Dudeism, Chilean correspondent for the *Dudespaper*.
- **Rev. Wendy Nixon** Contributor to the *Dudespaper* and Canadian correspondent.
- **Rev. Lisa Strouss** (Formerly known as Lisa Donald) Lebowski Studies innovator, published a thesis on Lebowski Theory, available at our Dude University (www.dudeuniversity.com), where she is an associate professor.

1. What do you think the philosophy of Dudeism can offer modern women?

Stella Quinn: Above all, Dudeism offers a fresh start. Being a religion without a deity, it allows us to come into this without any of the baggage monotheism has. Judaism, Christianity, Islam—these are all systems that worship The Man. Dudeists merely dig the style of the Dude. Big difference. The maleness of the monotheistic god has been used as an excuse to keep women under lock and key for thousands of years. Too many special ladies were excluded from the clergy and from proper education. Too many have been told what to wear, where they can go, and who they can have sex with because religion in general thinks that authority equals a pair of testicles.

Dudeism has no bearded dude in the sky telling you he loves you so much he can't wait to punish you. It just has a bearded Dude who is willing to go to your stupid dance recital. The Dude utterly rejects the restraints that conventional masculinity places on me. He exhibits none of the traits a man has been told are mandatory: to be financially successful, to be pointlessly brave, and to control the women in his life and his offspring. The Big Lebowski achieved all of these things, and he's a pathetic jerk. The Big Lebowski has a lot in common with popes, priests, and televangelists, with his crisp suit and symbolic seat of power. But his literal seat of power is one of weakness, and never once do we sympathize with him. Okay, except for maybe when Walter tosses the poor fucker on the floor.

The Dude's authenticity is nothing but good for women. Without male figures trying to control, manipulate, or own female bodies, women are free to be authentic and enjoy full status and participation. That kind of freedom is essential to feeling like a person. Dudeism offers women a way of thinking about the world that will never ask them to self-censor or conform to arbitrary gender roles. You're not going to see any neurotic casserole-baking Stepford Wives in this religion, because no Dudeist would ever cut a woman down like that.

Mother Duderior: To be more relaxed with life and every day's stresses and, therefore, be more confident with themselves, yet without being aggressive.

Andrea Maria Atenas: Being a woman in this time and place means fulfilling a lot of social expectations—rules meant to make us achieve, but in a wrong way. Those rules are not created to achieve self-fulfillment, so what happens to our soul and spirit?

There's too much of that whole *Sex and the City* thing goin' on, forcing us to think that we will find spiritual and mental peace through a pair of thousand-dollar shoes, or the latest fashion collection from some famous designer. That's a bummer, man.

Anyway, these days finding a place for the spirit has become more and more urgent. Some women may find it at a spa, in yoga, Prozac, or with their shrinks; but those are just moments, minutes of a day that won't give you necessarily an advanced philosophy on life, and most of the time, it's not collective but only self-serving. So it's necessary to find a place in which to find an everlasting peace of mind. That's what a modern woman can find through Dudeist philosophy—abide in good fellow Dudeships, or get advice about Dude-ifying your bathroom and making your own home spa.

Wendy Nixon: Dudeism provides a way to learn to just take it easy, man. Dudeism can be a portal into Oneness with Being. Maybe *tai chi* on the rug just doesn't do it for you. Adopting and practicing the philosophy of letting be is priceless for a woman caught in a patriarchal society. In other words, no matter how many carpet pissers cross our path, we can remain housebroken.

Lisa Strouss: While I feel that Dudeism is still an incarnation of male culture, a path of passive masculinity, I do believe the Way of the Dude can be applied to the feminist lifestyle. The way I see it, when you cannot find a path that suits you, you must make your own. For example, I consider myself to be a feminist, yet I cannot identify with gender-bender radicals, nor hyper-masculine females, or even those pale, skinny men leading the "Take Back the Night" marches on college campuses. Still, I consider the unspoken laws of gender culture to unconsciously dominate the way we behave in our lives and in society, and frankly, it is overwhelming. Makes me just want to kick back in my jelly sandals and watch it all pass me by, Dude-like, in my own way.

Let me just add that the Dude's jelly sandals are a testament to his pro-feminine doctrine, as the jelly sandal was perhaps the most coveted shoe of my childhood, and it was the first introduction for women of my generation to the concept of suffering for fashion. The shoes were painful, uncomfortable, sweaty, and blistering, and yet, you could not be considered a female contender on the social playground without them. When the Dude wears these shoes, I see him as a radical. It's almost like he's wearing a bra.

2. Do you think the feminist tradition is at odds with Dudeism, or are they compatible? Or are they secretly the same thing?

Stella Quinn: Feminism is a very important struggle, and it's done a helluva lot for our culture. The battle still isn't done in a lot of ways, because women are still second-class citizens in many parts of the world, and even in the West sexism is alive and well. Dudeism represents the end goal of feminism: to allow us all to just abide together without any labels to drive us apart. In this way, Dudeism also represents the state of mind we'll all have when we overcome bigotry in all its forms. To echo the words of the Great Dude John Lennon: "Imagine all the people, sharing all the world." That's what Dudeism is, and that's what feminism wants. The more Dudeists there are out there, the closer we bring feminism to its goal of not being needed any more.

Andrea Maria Atenas: It would be hard to understand why feminism wouldn't agree with Dudeism! Dudeism is a totally friendly philosophy. It points out all the aggressions that should not stand. Everybody can take comfort in that.

Also—and I'm talking about the Dude here—isn't he respectful toward women? Beyond being a man with a pair of testicles, he is a sympathizer with some feminist principles: He's against women being treated like objects, and when his lady friend wants to be a single mother without any moral judgment, he's happy to help her conceive—and without being a male chauvinist about it!

Finally, and maybe the most important, isn't Maude a perfect feminist icon?

Well, dudes, I think we can close the file on that one.

Wendy Nixon: What makes a feminist? Isn't thrusting your lack-of-johnson upon the world in an aggressive fashion pretty much the same thing as what the Brother Shamuses are doing? Dudeism is about letting every sentient being just *be*, as far as this Dude sees it. Many modern feminists insist that feminism isn't about aggressively supporting the female aspect and they take offence at the old, outdated view of hairy armpits and man-hating marches. Whatever. Honestly, I find the whole concept of being an "-ist" of any kind exhausting. I even only employ Dudeism to provide a frame of reference for my limber mind.

Lisa Strouss: It is hard for me to support the idea of a feminist tradition, as it seems that generationally, the feminist agenda changes and morphs to suit the needs of the present age and somehow remain very disconnected. I think socially people perceive feminists as some kind of secret society, where we all get together and vote and decide to set a precedent for all the devotees, but really, in this day, feminism is an isolated lifestyle, a choice made within the individual, for men and for women. Perhaps Dudeism *is* the new feminism, one that is without gender definition.

I feel like I'm already contradicting myself, but perhaps the characters are telling us that these notions of feminism and masculinity are no longer useful. Each man and each woman must define their approach to gender on their own terms according to the individual, and whatever they choose is right by nature of it being a self-defined path. And perhaps the closer we get to this genderless state, the more we see the social backlash and last grasps at antiquated gender ideologies.

Note the resurgence in youth culture of defining male and female territories: women turning cupcake-making and do-it-yourself dressmaking into boutique and high-end retail, young men growing beards and turning blue-collar clothes of America's labor past into expensive raw denim and luxury work boots. But this polarization cannot last—we each must find the male and female inside the self and accept both to be at peace. We must all become spiritual hermaphrodites.

3. Would it be harder for a woman to live her life like the Dude?

Stella Quinn: Certain aspects of the lifestyle would be more difficult to emulate, especially because women aren't full citizens just yet. Living alone in a Los Angeles apartment that is insanely easy to break into is not something most urban-dwelling ladies are gonna do. If a gal went to Ralphs in her jammies and robe to buy some half-and-half with a bad check, she'd probably get catcalled left and right. In fact, if you envision the plot of *The Big Lebowski* with a female protagonist, whole chunks of the movie would never have happened. Women have a lot more safety concerns than men do, and they have to do a lot more planning when moving around in public. Because of this they'd be less likely to turn up at random addresses to reclaim rugs or track down stolen cars without knowing how they'll be treated once they're in the door.

However, most aspects of the Dude's life would be easy-peasy to take on, such as taking a nice hot soak in the bath with candles all around for a little mood lighting. Hell, I did that way before I even heard of Dudeism. I think there's bigger stigma against men having candles in the bathroom at this point in our cultural history, where chicks are like, *expected* to have candles and other smelly shit all over the house. And finding a great rug that ties the room together? Hell, there's an entire industry pointed at women to help them out with that.

Bowling is an aspect of the Dude's lifestyle that appeals to everyone regardless of gender or background. Male, female, and mixed bowling leagues are all over the place. I suck way too much at throwing a straight rock to get involved with a league, but I enjoy the fine art of bumper bowling, especially since I don't have to put down my White Russian and try to aim.

Mother Duderior: I have no problems living as the Dude. Except for the fact that there are no bowling alleys in my area!

Andrea Maria Atenas: Dudeism is a state of mind, some spiritual state that can be admired and adopted by any person, regardless of their gender. We're all Dudes.

Wendy Nixon: I don't see why it need be. It might be slightly more difficult to find a special gentleman if you're strolling into Ralphs in your bathrobe, but that's hardly a hefty price to pay for the far-out, take-it-easy lifestyle.

Lisa Strouss: Only the Dude can be the Dude. It would be like asking the Dude to live his life like Maude. Or Walter to be like Bunny. We all must live according to our natures and allow others to do so without judgment, and without the bounds of gender ideologies that are no longer useful to the evolution of society.

4. Nominees for our Great Dudes in History are almost all male. Why do you think this is? Can you suggest any female Great Dudes in History?

Stella Quinn: Part of the problem is that, because humanity has been male-dominated for so long, a lot of special ladies never got the chance to shine out. Those that did had to be ruthless, making them resemble The Big Lebowski much more than the Dude.

Really, the greatest Dudes in History—male and female—are folks who never would have made the history books. The Dude certainly wouldn't be given a page in the books, yet, as the Stranger reminds us, there is something reassuring about knowing that he's out there abiding. The same goes for all the nameless women who have been swept under the rug while men wrote the history books. Catherine the Great, Cleopatra, Joan of Arc—sure, they're all impressive, but I feel better imagining a woman out of history who kept a tavern somewhere, brewed really kick-ass beer, and poured it out for weary travelers. There had to have been some special lady back in the Middle Ages, who, after losing a loved one, went to the local public house and ordered an oat soda from the landlady. The landlady would offer her condolences, and the special lady would admit her pain, but acknowledge that she's trying to abide. And somewhere else nearby, there's probably a Little Lebowski on the way. The truly great Dudes in History are nameless, and that's what helps us think of them as being yet another face of the Dude.

Mother Duderior: Um...a pair of testicles? To be a great woman often means that one has to overachieve. Which is often very un-Dude.

Andrea Maria Atenas: As we all know, women have been participating in world history for less time than men, and have only become major protagonists in the story recently. There were probably a lot of women getting things done through those hard times, but remained anonymous, and we may never know their stories.

I'd like to suggest Ella Fitzgerald as a great Dudeist because her life was quite difficult. She was abandoned by her father, her mother died, she grew up by herself, she faced the challenges of being a black woman in a racist society. However, her attitude was to give the world beauty in return.

Wendy Nixon: Nominees for pretty much anything in history are almost all male. Tell you what; you can put *me* down as a nominee and in a couple hundred years they'll all have someone to make statues of. Far-out.

Lisa Strouss: Well let me interpret that for myself: A great Dudeist woman is one who defines her own path without regard to gender definitions of the time. Virginia Woolf. Yayoi Kusama. Frances Farmer. Hedy Lamarr. Salome. And Oprah. I don't care what anyone says, I love Oprah.

5. Is *The Big Lebowski* more critical of traditional male roles or traditional female roles? Or are they equal?

Stella Quinn: *The Big Lebowski* takes no prisoners in its complete deconstruction of modern life. The Dude deflates masculine stereotypes in the Big Lebowski's speech about "what makes a man" with the puncturing truth that male genitalia is all that really makes a man a man. Maude eviscerates conventional femininity by being proud of her body, owning her sexuality, and allowing no man to control her. The union of Maude and the Dude represents humanity coming together after rejecting constraining and arbitrary gender roles, and the Little Lebowski is the hope for a post-gendered future.

Mother Duderior: What is equality anyway? Who wants to be the same as everyone else?

Wendy Nixon: I don't really see *The Big Lebowski* as critical of any role. From my perspective, it's a fantastic unfolding of karma, and each character reaps the benefits of their personal constitution. Even Donny, though I didn't like to see him go.

Lisa Strouss: The film does seem to satirize the archetypal feminist on one level, but I think that is really only a surface interpretation of the film. What do we experience symbolically beneath the dialogue of the characters? What roles are being played out socially? When you look at the "facts," the primary male characters have no social status and no finances. Even the so-called wealthy Lebowski has no true money of his own; he has only his [late] wife's money, nothing truly earned by his own labor.

The gender roles presented in the film seem to have no tradition really, although I do think it is very significant that Larry's father exists in a state of near-death in an iron lung. Because of his association with *Branded*, a show that reinforces the Western American male mystique, we are witnessing a literal death of that brand of masculinity. I have always felt that the secret of *The Big Lebowski* could be decoded in the Larry Sellers scenes. That if we studied Larry long enough, with spiritual devotion, the true meaning of the film would become clear.

6. What is your feeling about Maude, the film's heroine? Is she admirable or not?

Stella Quinn: Maude is a flawed heroine, but that's what makes her interesting. She couldn't be too perfect or she'd just be another feminine stereotype on film. Her independence and openness are impressive, but she's chock full of daddy issues that make her hard and sometimes petty. It's hard to believe that the loss of a single rug from the Lebowski household would really mean that much to someone so wealthy, but the rug becomes a very personal symbol of the contempt she feels for her father. The obsessive jealousy she shows toward Bunny doesn't help dispel stereotypes about female cattiness, and the plan she follows to secure the Dude as a sperm donor is so bizarre as to be pointless. Judging by the Dude's reaction when he discovers Maude's intention to conceive, it's very likely that all she would have had to do was ask straight up and he would have said yes.

The damage she exhibits shows that she's spent too much of her life living among manipulative, backstabbing assholes. It's only when she sheds the big green coat and gets some quality abiding in that we can see some vulnerability, and that finally humanizes her. Maude as a person is deeply flawed, but Maude as a character is extremely admirable in terms of what she does to alter the way women are usually presented on screen.

Mother Duderior: I liked Maude but not the company she keeps. Sometimes the arty crowd can be too arty. That and nondairy creamer sucks. Really sucks.

Andrea Maria Atenas: I dig her style! She has no need to wear high heels or nice lingerie to be more attractive and truly feminine. She is a real woman, a sort of Venus, maybe that's why she's always naked. Her image represents the original feminine beauty; I'm not talking about Eve here, I'm talking about Venus—there's something immaterial about her, something sublime. On a side note, I'm interested to know what she was laughing about in her conversation with Sandra and Knox. Were they laughing at the Dude?

Wendy Nixon: Maude appears comfortable in her own skin, with her artistic expression, and with her sexual and maternal needs. She seems clear, calm, and assertive without aggression (other than that knock on the jaw), and I think I'd enjoy her company in real life.

Lisa Strouss: Maude's weakness is her complete dismissal of the male role and her perception of the man to be simply biological, as a seed to produce the next generation. As women increase their power in society, it should not be to displace men. So why do we still perceive it in this way? Where did we learn this concept that one gender must dominate the other? So I think Maude is wrong to feel that fatherhood and male role models are no longer relevant. She is an extremist in this regard, but one cannot help but love and admire her creative dedication to the vaginal cause.

What about the Dude? Would you ever pair up with someone like him?

Stella Quinn: The Dude himself? Nah. I couldn't hang out with a guy who hung out with someone like Walter. But my boyfriend exhibits many Dudely characteristics, such as patience and an uncanny ability to roll with the punches. True self-confidence comes from neither caring what others think of you nor trying to impose your opinion on others. Guys who exhibit this most Dudely of traits are very, very sexy.

Mother Duderior: I am him! I abide! He looks better in shorts though.

Andrea Maria Atenas: With his spiritual sensitivity and that incredible Pendleton Cowichan sweater, why not?

Wendy Nixon: Yes. Someone so accepting of others and their individual idiosyncrasies is highly attractive. He takes each day, situation, event, and catastrophe as they come, employs the necessary means to deal with them, and enjoys the adventure of it all. He's motivated enough to maintain shelter, to keep his belly full and his mind limber, and to drive around and bowl. Sounds like a fantastic special gentleman to me.

Lisa Strouss: You know what, I've dated many incarnations of the Dude. I've been that Special Lady. And unfortunately, I have to say, I've outgrown him. I respect him, but I think he's a bit of a self-indulgent alcoholic and at this point in my life, I'd rather be with the porn director, because at least he's employed.

8. What changes would you like to see in Dudeism to make it appeal more to women?

Stella Quinn: In essentials, Dudeism has everything it needs to appeal to women. All it will need is to maintain awareness of how it represents gender. As long as nothing is done to alienate or marginalize women, plenty of special ladies will join the ranks. This same idea applies to all groups that have experienced marginalization in mainstream culture—non-whites and sexual minorities come to mind. As long as Dudeism avoids labeling individual people, we'll all just be Dudes. The second any one label gains privilege over the rest, we'll have lost our core ethos and turned into the mainstream society we've rejected.

Mother Duderior: Eeep! Um...more jewelry?

Andrea Maria Atenas: I don't want to be sycophant, but I think it's perfect.

Lisa Strouss: I don't think Dudeism should change in any way. If it must change, the evolution will happen naturally. I don't think it needs to appeal more to women. It either does or it doesn't. I believe Dudeism was a gift to men, the American appropriation of Zen culture. It is a way to pass down the teachings so that we might understand them through contemporary symbols. Dudeism is there for those who seek it, man or woman. To be a Dudeist missionary goes against the way of the Dude.

9. The spiritual state of Dudeness is called "abiding." What techniques do you employ in your day-to-day life that help you to abide?

Stella Quinn: I've always been very into music. I obsessively groom my music collection on my laptop so I can easily create playlists that echo the mood of the day. I also play a few instruments and particularly enjoy unwinding with my ukulele. Yoga is also everything it's cracked up to be. After a good yoga workout, nothing in my body hurts anymore and the world just feels a bit more peaceful.

Lately I've taken to journaling my thoughts on the verses of the *Tao Te Ching*. The translation by Jonathan Star is really something special, and reading just a few sentences will spawn paragraphs of thought. Writing my thoughts out with paper and ink, just for myself, has helped me combat the overwhelmed feeling I can get from the fast-paced, fully connected digital world I have to operate in every day.

I also have a bat-shit crazy cat named Loki that really helps me with the Zen thing. Cats are critters that exist in a world outside of time. Having a little purring fur-ball curled up for a nap on your lap can really help you reset your priorities.

Mother Duderior & Andrea Maria Atenas: Mind if I burn a jay?

Wendy Nixon: Dudeism for me was a gateway to a greater seeing. Learning to let go and allow greater forces than myself (relatively speaking) handle the big things and the little things was incredibly helpful to my daily mental state. Abiding is also actually the key factor in "successful" meditation. Many people cannot stop their mind when they meditate. The trick is, don't *try* to stop it. Just…abide it, man. Let the mind do what it wants, and just be aware that you are *the Dude*, not the mind. Ultimately, the greatest state of oneness and peace is attainable through abiding. And true abiding comes when you realize you never really had any control over any of it to start with. The Dude abides. And all is the Dude.

Lisa Strouss: Abiding is a wonderful approach to the great melodrama of our lives. We cannot control what happens to us; we can only control our reaction. Abiding is to allow life to happen to us without resistance, to embrace the unknown, to accept others, and to accept ourselves. Abiding is also to let go. Letting go of what we think should happen, or what we want to happen, and allowing life to surprise us. Every day I fearlessly freefall into my life with total acceptance. That is how I abide.

III

Making It to Practice— Dudeist Lifestyle and Techniques

SELF-HELP CHOPPERIN' IN

The Dudeism Helping to Abide Movement (DHAM)

Traditional religion can no longer provide answers to our big questions about "life, the universe, and everything." So when it comes to finding solace in a world that seems to have gone crazy, people are increasingly left to their own devices.

Unfortunately, as we've pointed out, those devices are usually exactly that—devices. That is, technological gadgets designed to distract us momentarily from despair. You know, for kids. They've produced exciting things in hyperactive electronic ware: iPods, TVs, computer porn, and video games. Wave of the future, dude—100 percent electronic. And ultimately, 100 percent unsatisfying. But then, that's the point—consumer culture isn't designed to satisfy us or provide lasting contentment. If it did, their revolution would be over and the bums would win.

In 1955, a famous marketing strategist wrote:

Our enormously productive economy demands
that we make consumption our way of life, that we
convert the buying and use of goods into rituals, that
we seek our spiritual satisfactions, our ego satisfac-
tions, in consumption. The measure of social status,
of social acceptance, of prestige, is now to be found
in our consumptive patterns. The very meaning and
significance of our lives today expressed in consump-
tive terms.

His name? Victor Lebow. Is there a literal connection here? Well dude, we just don't know.[43] Fortunately, gadgets and other stuff aren't the only substitutes for the content-ment that religion once provided. Philosophical books like this one have long been keeping minds limber in order to make sense of the whole durn human comedy. And this prob-ably explains why the subset of the book-publishing industry with the highest earnings is called "Self-Help."

These self-help folks we wanna tell you about, they call themselves the Self-Help and Actualization Movement, or SHAM for short. Now, SHAM, that's not an acronym anyone would self-apply where we come from, but there's a lot about the Self-Help and Actualization Movement that doesn't make a lot of sense to us.

For instance, we're puzzled by its relative ineffective-ness. Studies show that self-help books, videos, tapes, and other of their published tools and techniques rarely impose any positive or long-lasting change on people's lives. In his book *SHAM: the Self-Help and Actualization Movement*, Steve

---

43 See: http://bit.ly/6wGeVr.

Salerno fucks the SHAMmers in the EST by suggesting that—like the "religion" of consumerism that predated it—the entire movement is a fraudulent money-making scheme intentionally devoid of any actual ability to help anyone. In other words, self-help books are just gadgets meant to distract us momentarily, to be consumed and thrown away. Are you surprised at his sneers?

Don't be. The practice of purchasing peace of mind has long been a central part of human spirituality. This is what the religions of old warned us about: Icon worship, dude. Or perhaps, "iCons," in the parlance of our ™s.

So what—Salerno thinks the capitalist pigsters did this? It's all a goddamn fake? Is it like Lenin said? We are the Wal-marts? Well dude, we just don't know. After all, when it

comes to the self-help community, we'll allow there are some nice folks out there. But there are also plenty of dipshits, fucking amateurs, human paraquat, and goddamn morons looking to make an easy buck by capitalizing on the misery of the masses. You…you…*human therapyquat!*

As an antidote to the idea that self-help is composed primarily of creeps who can fucking roll in it, we present our own humble contribution to the SHAM corpus of thought. Basically, these are Dudeist reinterpretations of some of their most well-known books. But don't take them too seriously. We're not trying to SHAM anyone here, man. We just think that most of people's self-help needs can be transmitted by watching *The Big Lebowski*. It is our most modestly priced receptacle. From religion to consumerism to self-help to Dudeism. Down through the pages, across the ampersands of time. We dropped off the DHAM money.

The following are summaries of take-it-easy manuscripts that are not yet finished. We've got four more detectives down at the lab working on the case. Got 'em working in flip-flops.

The Seven Spiritual Laws of Takin' 'Er Easy

Deepak Chopra's most famous book, *The Seven Spiritual Laws of Success*, may not have been the first self-help guide to conflate "spirituality" with financial success, but it was the first one clever enough to stick them together in the title. As you'll see in all our self-help books below, choosing a snappy title is half the game. After coming up with a great title, a self-help book practically writes itself. Hey, that's probably one of the spiritual laws. Anyway, here's a summary of the Dudeist version of Chopra's ground-breaking book:

1. The Law of Not Doing Anything

In *Doing Nothing: A History of Loafers, Loungers, Slackers, and Bums in America*, Tom Lutz wrote extensively and painstakingly about not doing anything. The book is almost 400 pages long, and writing it must have been exhausting. But the author did have a point. And it was a good one—that no one does nothing forever. Not until they're dead, anyway. The fear of doing nothing (or failure or inertia or boredom or depression) could be seen as a close cousin to the fear of death. But don't be worried about that shit! Life literally goes on, man. Rest assured (or just rest) that eventually you'll have to get up off the couch. Or else you really will be dead. Once you realize this, you can stop worrying and relax completely. Then you'll discover that truly doing nothing is one of life's greatest pleasures.

2. The Law of Making It to Practice

They say "practice makes perfect." But who wants to be perfect? For some of us, years of math classes and piano lessons and shit like that have rendered the word "practice" rather unappealing. What they don't tell you is that if it's something you love to do, practice is just another word for "play." And the more you play something, the more you dig its style. In that case, the pleasure comes not from making it to the finals, but from realizing that "it's just a game, man" and that you're lucky to get a lane in the first place. Don't think about whether you're going to enter the next round-robin or not. This is not your homework, Larry. This is a league game.

3. The Law of Being There, Man

There are so many strands in our heads these days, man. It's a complicated case, this life. We're always trying to make it better, to figure it all out. But it's never going to get better because we'll always be looking to take the next hill. And we'll never figure it out because when you figure one thing out, another complicated case pops up. So sometimes you've got to just say, "Fuck it," and just go bowling or just sit back and watch the cycle. When the Dude tells his landlord "I'll be there, man" he means it. He really will take in the whole "cycle," every bizarre gesture, no matter how ludicrous the story may seem to be. He'll try to dig the style, even if he doesn't know what the fuck is going on. As Woody Allen suggested, "Eighty percent of success is just showing up."

4. The Law of Laziness

What the Taoists call *wu wei*, we call Dude Way. It is the principle that by doing what comes easy to you, you'll get things done without wasting excess energy or trying too hard. This is also known as the 80-20 principle (though Dudeists call it the "Mark it Eight Principle"). The 80-20 principle says that 20 percent of your actions lead to 80 percent of your results. So what you do is, figure out which is which, then only do the

20 percent and blow off the other 80. That way you can bump yourself into a higher lax bracket![44]

5. The Law of Those Are the Fucking Rules

In the 20th century, nihilists came up with the idea that there were no rules to give a shit about. It sounded like a good idea, but they didn't do very well at it. People need rules, man. Without rules, this sentence could not exist. Nothing could exist. Everything would be face down in the muck, if not muck itself. That's why Walter, a devout Jew, prefers Nazis over nihilists. "At least it's an ethos," he says. Though Nazis did some horrible shit, if nihilists were in charge, things would likely become far worse.

The reason that it's popular these days to disregard rules or flagrantly break them is because a lot of the time the rules we have to follow are bad ones thought up by real reactionaries only looking out for the one who will benefit (themselves). That's why it's important to know when to break the rules. Here's a simple answer to tattoo on your forehead: Break the rules when it doesn't hurt anybody else.

When Smokey's toe slips over the line a little, Walter points a gun at him, enforcing the rules. But Smokey's not toeing the line exactly is hardly a police matter. The Dude

---

44 For a practical guide on how to incorporate the 80-20 principle in your life, see *The Four-Hour Workweek* (the section "Pareto and His Garden"), by Tim Ferriss. Ferriss' objective is to work four hours a week and make a shitload of money. That in mind, we should assume that one could work one hour a week or less and make enough to cover basic expenses. Maybe we can apply the 80-20 principle to the 80-20 principle itself, and arrive at the 96-4 principle?

reminds us that rules are sometimes fuzzy around the edges. Rules help us take 'er easy by not having to think so much and to get along with each other, but when they make life too complicated or painful, they need to reject prior restraint.

6. The Law of Fucking Listening Occasionally

The problem with some lazy people is that they can be so often lost in daydream sequences that they miss out on real life. Daydreams are of vital importance to the Dudeist mind-set and lifestyle, but they can also fuck up the most simple plan if they prevent us from paying attention. The trick is to know when to fucking listen occasionally and learn something and when to say, "Fuck it," or "I'm sorry, I wasn't listening." There is so much to listen to these days that it's important to take the time to go in, tune out, and kick back. Otherwise, all the strands in ol' Duder's head will get tangled up and make him or her very un-Dude. But not listening at all will turn you into a goddamn moron or a fucking dunce.

7. The Law of Achieving the Modest Task Which is Your Charge

Ah fuck it, six laws is enough.

Fuggedaboud the Funny Shtuff

In *Don't Sweat the Small Stuff (And It's All Small Stuff)*, Richard Carlson encouraged everyone to stop worrying about all the irrelevant shit that we tend to stress out about in our lives. Unfortunately, the "small stuff" is the stuff of which lives are made, and people just can't resist getting all wrapped up in it no matter how many books with platitudinous titles you write. Why is that?

Kurt Vonnegut said that the reason people are so keen to fuck up their lives is because they've seen too many fairy tales. People see soap operas, the *Jerry Springer Show*, or movies and think that their own lives are supposed to be full of drama. So they latch on to all the small stuff in their lives and inflate things way out of proportion, picking fights, or doing shitty things to people close to them. Or they feel like they have to "shake things up," because that's what they've learned from the way Hollywood and reality TV fixates on all the petty stuff in life and makes it luridly entertaining.

However, the fictional stories we enjoy are only a small portion of the lives of their characters. What you don't see are the repercussions afterward—of how small stuff begets more small stuff to worry about: after the dramatic love story, the boring marriage that ends in divorce. After the rise to the top of fame and fortune, the hero has to contend with bad investments and bickering with family members. After finding the golden ring and bringing it back to the village, the whole village getting sacked and burned by a jealous neighboring tribe. All those characters ultimately find themselves saying, "This whole fucking thing. I could have just had pee stains on my rug." But they don't show that part.

The Big Lebowski, while showing many characters who are caught up in the drama of the small stuff in their lives, features a character who does his best to fuggedaboud all the unimportant funny shtuff that most folks usually worry about. The Dude's story baffles a lot of moviegoers because he doesn't achieve anything in the film. Yet, what he achieved *wasn't* shown in the movie: not financial success or a hot trophy wife, but a peaceful and placid trophy life. The goal of the Dude is not achievement, but peace of mind. When we re-orient ourselves to see the world through his shades, it may seem less bright and loud and thrilling than the movies, but it's a lot more pleasant overall.

So, whereas *Don't Sweat the Small Stuff* featured a list of strategies to get ahead in life, *Fuggedaboud the Funny Shtuff* teaches you to stop trying to live your life like a movie. Can't be worried about that shit. Life goes on, man. Movies end after 90 minutes.

Limberal Thinking

Ed De Bono popularized the term "lateral thinking" back in the '70s, around the time of our trouble with the Vietnamese. Lateral thinking was meant to be a more creative way of using our brains than the strict, linear, and hierarchical mode that most people were familiar with. When the Dude says that his "thinking about this case has become very uptight" but concedes that "fortunately I'm adhering to a strict drug regimen to keep my mind limber," he's talking about this kind of thinking. Of course, drugs can be considered optional.

So this here limberal thinking we wanna tell you about is lateral thinking plus the Dude's "limber thinking" plus "limbic thinking." What's Limbic Thinking? Some kind of limbo thing? Far from it. Limbic refers to the limbic system, a part of the brain associated with motivation, emotion, and the senses.

See, the thing about lateral thinking is that it deals exclusively with concepts. Limberal thinking deals with impressions and feelings as well. The Dude thinks with his whole body. People forget that the brain is the biggest erogenous zone. You've heard of emotional intelligence? Call this dudemotional intelligence. It's where all the interested parties (body, feelings, thinking) meet, in bed with everyone, playing one side against the other. Fabulous stuff.

Not many learned men have disputed this. But that's because we just thought of it. Anyway, it's a field of study for smarter fellers than ourselves to officially investigate. We don't remember much from college.

Ironic Jeff

In 1990, famed poet Robert Bly wrote *Iron John: A Book About Men*, which asked the big question of *The Big Lebowski*, namely: "What makes a man?" Only Bly meant it more literally—what can men do to truly become men?

As a response to the "soft male" who was supposedly in touch with his feminine side at the cost of his masculine, Bly's *Iron John* was also an attempt to initiate males from boys into a traditional form of manhood.

While the soft male (or "girly men," as Neanderthal Arnold Schwarzenegger derisively called them) hasn't much been in vogue since Alan Alda's persona in the '70s, eternal youths who refuse to grow up seem to be a big problem today. Beginning in the '90s (around the time when *The Big Lebowski* was set), Bly and other self-help authors like Dan Kiley (*The Peter Pan Syndrome*) have been goading guys to grow up and be men. Even wacky Judd Apatow movies are ultimately complicit in this criticism—after celebrating freewheeling overgrown adolescents for 75 minutes, Apatow's stories always wrap things up with the man-boys tossing the bong aside to become pillars of their community.

The message is clear—grow up, get a job, get married, and have kids, or you'll end up a deadbeat, a loser, someone the square community doesn't give a shit about.

However, for those with the dudetermination and fortidude to do so, not "growing up" in the traditional sense may well be a hee-roic and excellent adventure on the order of Bill and Ted. See, for most of history, not growing up meant that you literally wouldn't grow up—in other words, you'd probably die. And so would everyone else. Life was hard, and men had to pull their weight by doing exactly what their fathers did, including killing animals and rival humans. Things, of course, are different today. Men (and women too) still need to work and compete a bit, but unlike in our primitive days, we can be anything we'd like to be and competition is a lot friendlier. And the very nature of our social reality is changing ever more rapidly. Remember that in 1990 the Dude had probably not even heard of the internet.

Bly's prescription for men to embrace their dark, violent, and bloody side in order to become "whole" is like saying that women need to give birth to babies to be complete women. We may have some biological baggage and instinct lying dormant, but that doesn't mean we have to awaken it to feel good. Bly disparages the increasing numbers of men who refuse to grow up, labeling them "fly boys." A protégé of Sigmund Freud, Marie Von Franz, disparagingly labeled them *puer aeternus.* This is all very ironic, since "flight" and "eternal youth" have been two of humankind's most long-standing desires. Yet until the Dude came along, these free birds of youth had very few respectable and resolute role models.

Disciples of Bly had Iron John urging them to revive some kind of primordial masculinity from the Iron Age when men had to grow up, forge tools, and kill things. But in this postmodern Age of Irony, we Dudeists choose instead to align ourselves with Ironic Jeff. Exemplifying how to just take it easy, man, Jeff "Dude" Lebowski helps us look at life with humorous, lighthearted affection instead of viewing it as something beastly to attack with sharp sticks. The Dude is

UPCOMING TITLES

The Power of Spliff (*The Power of Myth*)

How to Befriend Losers and Influential People (*How to Win Friends and Influence People*)

Man's Search for Meeting (*Man's Search for Meaning*)

Dudenetics/Abidentology (Dianetics/Cybernetics/Scientology)

The Power of Positive Thankie (*The Power of Positive Thinking*)

Awaken the Pliant Within (*Awaken the Giant Within*)

Learned Slobtimism (*Learned Optimism*)

DudEST (The EST Movement)

The Sellerstine Prophecy (*The Celestine Prophecy*)

Secret Shit Has Come to Light (*The Secret*)

For more Dudeist self-help books, or to suggest ideas to us, please visit our site: dudeism.com/DHAM.

truly the man for this time and place. And we can be as well, should we choose The Road Less Rambled.

The Road Less Rambled

M. Scott Peck borrowed a line incorrectly attributed to Robert Frost—"The Road Not Taken" in his 1978 book *The Road Less Traveled*—to describe the difficulty and value of the spiritual path. Dudeism agrees with Peck, only we're not sure that spirituality has to be a slog.

Taoism would suggest that the spiritual path should be the easiest—once we realize which direction the flow is going, we can take 'er easy and float along with the current. The hard part isn't in the rambling—it's in staying out of the way of all the other dipshits struggling to plow against the current. As a result, the spiritually adept must find his refuge from society, either in his or her private residence, or by living away from the "madding crowds." He or she must avoid temples and testaments of the un-Dude—shopping malls, television commercials, fashion, technological fetishism, and so on.

To go with the flow, you have to go against the grain. As we've said, it's no easy thing to take it easy. There's just so much pressure from the square community, from our compeers, and from those in charge of scheduling, to make everything harder than it needs to be.

The Power of Not Now

Eckhart Tolle became something of an overnight sensation after his book *The Power of Now* was published in 1999. It's an alternately inspiring and confounding book that bounces willy-nilly between rational common sense and presumptuous New-Ageism.

We've got nothing against Tolle, and consider him rather Dudely indeed, but we'd like to follow his exegesis on "living in the moment" with a modest addition: "lounging in the moment."

When most self-help books tell you to "live in the moment," their intention is to free you from any remorse of the past and anxiety about the future. Far out. The only problem is that this is all easier said than done—no one seems to know how to do it. Ironically, one of the most popular new-age prescriptions is called "creative visualization," where you imagine whatever you'd like to have in your life and "manifest" it. But this makes no sense—what is more prone to prevent you from living in the moment than imagining stuff you'd like to have in the future? Don't be fatuous, Ecky. The theory is ludicrous.

So we offer this simpler and more sensible solution instead: creative procrastination. The power of *not now*. The way to live in the moment is to make a list of all the things you *should* do, and then not do them. Enjoy the sudden freedom from pressure and responsibility as you shirk your duties with conscious determination! Relax and let your mind wander, and new pathways are likely to open up in front of your imagination without raising your blood pressure one bit.

When you finally decide to get up momentously from the couch, it will be not because you should, but because dudey calls, and you're good and ready to take that hill.

DUDERINOS UNANIMOUS

A 12-Step Program for Personal Dudevolution

We're not sure why personal improvement programs always require 12 steps. Nevertheless, Alcoholics Anonymous pioneered the idea of the 12-step program and our version is inspired by theirs. Our goal is similar to theirs, but instead of trying to overcome alcohol or narcotic addiction, the Duderinos Unanimous program is much more general, designed to help us be more "Dude" from day to day.

1. Admit that the whole world has gone crazy. We may be powerless over it. But we can take care of our own private residence.

"A journey of a thousand miles begins with a single step," or so goes the Zen adage. Sometimes the greatest journey of all can begin by doing the opposite—by refusing to take any more steps. After so many people telling us what we should do to make our lives better, the most dramatic act of self-improvement can be to stop "trying" to do anything. Once we realize, "It's all a game," man, we can relax and get a less uptight view on the whole case.

2. Believe there is a Dude Way to the universe.

Dudeism is a nontheistic religion, but that doesn't mean we don't believe there's something tying "it all" together. At least on the humanistic level, the idea that there is a natural and harmonious way in which life unfolds is not only an important part of Taoism, but is increasingly being suggested

by science—via disciplines like evolutionary psychology, complexity theory, chaos theory, and other far-out new shit that's currently coming to light. Although academics may say everything is relative, and some mystics say that life is all an illusion, the idea that there is a "high road" is at the very least a useful idea that can help us feel at home in the world, or at least in our own little corner of it.

3. Be determined to follow the Dude Way. And to follow it further on down the trail.

One of the reasons we can end up ushering un-Dudeness into our lives is because everything is so complicated. By consciously following the Dude Way and practicing Dudeist techniques, we can help simplify things and make sense of where we're going.

4. Where's the meaning, Lebowski? It's down there somewhere, take another look.

By always being skeptical and always pursuing meaning rather than material, we will bring a limberness to our minds that can roll with any gutterball and deal with all the dings and dipshits that may come our way. It is only when we feel unattached[45] that we abide; without strings, the world can't drag us along with it when it goes fucking crazy.

---

45 In the Buddhist sense of the word. Though almost everyone has "strings" (responsibilities to family, friends, jobs, etc.) Buddhism says we shouldn't be "attached" to the outcomes or expectations of those relationships.

5. Say, "Fuck it." That's your answer for everything.

Again, by leaving the strands in our heads unknotted, we can easily let them go. If things don't work out, then leave them alone. We can try to tie it up sometime down the trail when things get easier. No sense wasting energy now when you can do things more efficiently later. (See "Self Help Chopperin' In," page 177.)

6. Take long baths and meditate on your rug.

The ethos of modern civilization is "Just do it," but the Dudeist's is rather the opposite: "Just don't do it," or even better, "Just dude it." To do nothing takes courage and discipline, but in the end, the struggle will be worth it, resulting in greater peace of mind and appreciation for the simple things in life. This will not happen overnight! A lifetime of business papers cannot be towed away in an instant. What are you not waiting for? Don't do it now!

7. What in God's holy name are they blathering about? That's just like their opinions, man.

Lots of people will tell you that you're crazy for following the Dude Way. Remember that you're not the follower of a crazy cult—they are. Just because there are more people in their cult doesn't mean theirs is better. Also, have compassion for them—they know not what they undude. Your easygoing lifestyle is a threat to their entire worldview. But down deep they're just uptight bullies, going around blaming you for the fact that life isn't fair. They have their story, you have yours.

8. Be Dude to everyone you meet.

There is no reason, there's no FUCKING reason why you should ever be un-Dude to anyone. You'll never derive any benefit from being a fucking asshole. Even when pederasts curse at you, or officers of the law make fun of you, maintain an easygoing attitude. People are afraid to be nice to strangers because they might look stupid. But stupidity is in the "I" (ego) of the beholder. Anyone who doesn't appreciate your friendliness probably doesn't deserve it in the first place.

9. Be there, man.

In the immortal words of "righteous dude" Ferris Bueller, "Life moves pretty fast. If you don't stop to look around once in a while, you could miss it." The art of living is practiced on a day-to-day basis. Say what you will about the tenets of painting, dance, music, and filmmaking—there is no higher art than the one you doodle with your *existencil*. Be as proud of the canvas you paint every day as you would of one they'd hang in the Louvre.

10. Stop making illiteral connections.

The Dude minds his mind, man. That's because we are not our minds. Minds can be real worthy fucking adversaries— always making us feel bad or confused or down in the dumps. And they can trick us into thinking everything has something to do with Vietnam. Adopting a cool, rational and detached attitude about everything can help us appreciate life instead of being frightened of it. Hey...nice marmot!

11. Adhere to a strict drug regimen to keep your mind limber.

While the Dude advocates external drug use both in action and words, he means them only as a vehicle to greater understanding, not escape from the world.

Though drugs have been demonized over the past few decades, we need to acknowledge that we are in fact on drugs all the time—our brains are constantly injecting serotonin, dopamine, adrenaline, opiates, and other natural forms of junk into our veins and our brains. To try to moderate this via meditation, conscious behavior, and sometimes even some well-chosen external chemicals, is akin to cooking—we just need to get the recipes right to avoid suffering (mental) health problems.

Of course, drugs aren't necessary to get high. We can get all fucked up on life just by learning to see our lives as an acid flash-forward. By developing the powers of our imagination through regular, determined daydreaming, reading, thinking, and other psychedelic pursuits, we can dramatically enrich the quality of our lives. Of course, like the real reactionaries and their pharma-illlogical lines in the sand, we too should differentiate these "good drugs" from the "bad drugs" upon which most of our population is heavily addicted: TV, consumerism, nonstop entertainment, violence, and status-seeking.

12. Spread the Dude word.

The cool thing about Dudeism in general—and *The Big Lebowski* in particular—is that it's a great shibboleth. "Shibboleth" is a word from Biblical times that was hard for some people to pronounce and so was used as a sort of test to see if they were actually members of your "league" or not.

In helping to spread the Dude word, you're bound to find other like-minded compeers, you know? The world can be a dark place if you don't have others around who dig your style. What's more, you might even help "save" borderline assholes, fascists, dipshits, real reactionaries, and human paraquat who might be looking for an excuse to stand up (or lie down) and join the Dude movement. Cast a chill upon the world, dude. And make it feel all warm inside as a result. *Halle-Dude-Yeah*! Fuckin' A, man.

To officially take the Duderinos Unanimous vow, please visit: dudeism.com/duderinos.

DUDEITATION

Just Drop in to See What Condition Your Condition Is In

It's easy to criticize the Dude for being lazy. But criticizing the Dude for being lazy—well, that's just downright lazy in itself! It ignores the fact that the Dude's lifelong laziness is actually a difficult thing to pull off. So few of us are able to be as effectively laid-back as the Dude. It would take years of diligent training for us to begin to approach his Olympic–level of indolence.

Though the Stranger introduces the Dude by saying he's "quite possibly the laziest man in Los Angeles county, which would place him high in the running for laziest worldwide," he's either being fatuous or it's just that he's never been to England or France, or anyplace else with a socialist work ethic (none) or a culture focused primarily around drinking with friends. Moreover, anyone who's been to Los Angeles would never apply the handle "easygoing" to it.

Truth is, there are countless men and women around the world far lazier than the Dude. In fact, the laziest among them have actually made a career out of their laziness. And it's the lifestyle of these ingenious goldbricking bums that we want to innerduce you to in this chapter.

Like the Dude, the careers of these deadbeats have slowed down a little. But that's only because their careers are all about slowing down a little. Perhaps you've heard about these folks—they're called monks. Every religion has them, not just the Irish ones. Of course, you don't hear about them much because they're generally too lazy to go on TV and yell into microphones, or write bestsellers, or maintain websites or charity foundations, or initiate jihads, or hold bake sales. Despite what most folks think, being a monk is not just about going without sex and drugs and reality TV. The Dude has sex and drinks and smokes pot, but he is still in many regards a modern-day holy man. That's because, like his more ortho-dox religious brethren, his primary occupation is to spend his days worshipping. Only he worships and pays obeisance not to God, but to life itself.

Instead of separating the clergy (religious suit-wearing workers) from the monkhood (religious robe-wearing slack-ers) as other religions do, Dudeism contends that everyone should bring a little monk into their lives. We gotta feed the "monky"! As in the Dude's life, there's still time to bowl, drive around, and enjoy the occasional acid flashback, but the most sacred time is when you create some sacred space, recharge your batteries, and indulge in some lucid (or even lurid) dream sequences. Makes you feel all warm inside, ties all the strands in your head together. And afterward, it sure makes it easier to take it easy when you come down from your bungalow-on-high and enter a world of pain.

The key to feeding the monky, to bringing a little monk-hood into your 'hood, is a little technique called "dudei-tation." And though new-age magazines and gurus and publishing companies might not agree, you don't need any special instructions or teaching to learn how to dudeitate. It's like bowling. In fact, in many ways it's exactly like bowl-ing. You can figure it out for yourself, and though you might suck at first, the more you do it, the better you get. But you have to be relaxed about it or you'll never properly learn to dig its style.

Sure, some of those dudeitators you might have seen don't look all that relaxed: Their backs are as straight as the proverbial rod (or johnson), and their legs are twisted in

AN INNERDUCTION TO LOOSENING YOUR TRAIN OF THOUGHT

1. *Find somewhere comfortable.* On the floor, on the sofa, in a recliner, in the tub, etc. Just make sure you're comfortable. Also make sure it's quiet. And that no one can disturb you. Turn the sound off on your answering machine. Lock the door. Take extra care if you have an outward-opening door on your house.

2. *Close your eyes and do not think. Also, do not* not *think.* What the fuck am I talking about? See, if you try *not* to not think, you'll find yourself thinking about how you're thinking about not thinking. The dance, you know, the cycle? It can really give you a rash. So just watch your thoughts and let them drift by pleasantly like magic carpets in the sky. Do not give yourself notes. Remember, you're like a child who wanders into the middle of a movie. Don't try to figure out what

wilder positions than you'd find in a Jackie Treehorn movie. But the Dude shows us that we can dudeitate in any situation or position we choose: while doing *tai chi* with a White Russian in one hand; while lying on the rug, listening to four-year-old audio tapes of bowling tournaments; while sitting in the tub smoking a jay; and while listening to tapes of whales bleating in the background. In short, there are infinite ways to dudeitate because dudeitation is not something you do. It's something you *don't* do.

Don't do, dude? What in Dude's holy name are we blathering about? Well, I'll tell you what I'm blathering about. I've got certain information, man. *Wu wei* has come to light.

anything means or what's the fucking point. There is none, nor is there any literal connection.

3. *Don't worry about doing this for any set length of time.* Just sit there (or lie there, or hang there, or what-have-you there) until you think you've done enough. Lots of dudeitators make a big deal about how long they can dudeitate. That must be exhausting. But this isn't a league game, man. Ten minutes can be fine. Even one minute can help you say, "Shut the fuck up, Brainy!"

4. *Now go out and achieve anyway.* It's your roll. You have the necessary means, necessary means for a higher level of consciousness.

5. *Make sure to make it to practice.* But how often you dudeitate is up to you. Have it your way, dude. I know that you will.

For more Dudeitation tips, please visit: dudeism.com/dudeitation.

There's a principle in Eastern religion and philosophy that the Taoists call *wu wei*, but which can be found in Buddhism and Hinduism as well. *Wu wei* literally means "not-do" and can be translated as "doing by not doing" or "doing without trying." The idea is this: There is a natural flow to things, and the Dude among us will ride that flow and allow it to drop us where we need to be.

The un-Dude, on the other hand will struggle against the current, doing things the hard way, making waves wherever they go, crashing into everyone headed downstream, and generally churning things up so that the clarity and peacefulness of our surroundings is lost. They will do this out of impatience or to hold fast to some desired course of action or ideal outcome. They're not wrong, exactly; they're just assholes.

Sound like someone we know? Someone who forces Vietnam into every conversation, who makes "fool-proof" plans that fuck everything up, who pulls his piece out on the lanes because someone's toe slipped over the line? In short, dudeitation is a way to get our inner Walter to just take it easy and shut the fuck up so that the Dude can take the wheel.

Of course, as we've said, it's not easy to "not do" things. We've been told our whole lives, "Don't just sit there, do something." But too often the opposite is best: "Don't just do something, sit there." The Dude and other funky monks like himself are masters of the latter. Why? Because they know that life is not all about action. It's also about being. Do-be-do-be-do, dude. Our society has sorely neglected the value of one to the detriment of the other. And it takes both in equal measure to make life a whole durn human comedy.

What meditation does is teach us how to "not do" by literally practicing how not to do it. Any meditator can tell you, the more you try to meditate, the harder it is to do. You have to just let it happen without interference. It's the ultimate irony, isn't it? And yet it's the basis of all creative effort, from coitus to painting to figuring out a complicated case. It is the essence of the limber mind, it is a strict drug regimen, and the drug is life itself. Mind if I do a do-be?

Although it's hilarious that the Dude meditates blissfully to a tape of an old bowling tournament, it's also an incredibly profound and effective way to prepare for a tournament.

By placing himself in the context of a stressful situation and allowing himself to relax and feel good about it, the Dude will know how to remain calm when he really does have to face off against worthy fucking adversaries. Although the Dude sometimes gets frazzled and becomes "verrry un-Dude," as Walter happily points out, we all can learn from how quickly he settles back into his abidingly calm center while cruising life's proverbial rocky ride. "Can't be worried about that shit! Life goes on!" he says after losing a million dollars and his car, and being threatened with castration. By all accounts, it's the same with world-class meditators: They might start worrying about shit, but not for long; they quickly catch themselves before darkness warshes over and there is no bottom.

There's a lot to like about the Dude. But there's one thing that stands out above all the rest: his calm, collected character in the face of catastrophe. Don't we all wish we could be a little more Dude in similar situations? Or even in far less worrisome ones? However, if the Dude's private life is anything to go on, he wasn't born that way—it took years of "making it to practice" to make him the enlightened-up Dude that he is.

Wave of the present, dude. Surf the bosom of the Pacific.

THIS AGGRESSION WILL NOT STAND

Dude-Jitsu, the Dudeist Art of Self-Defense

"The effect of tightening up on the mind is
to make it unfree."
—*Takuan Soho, Zen monk*

"What the fuck are you thinking?"
—*The Dude*

The martial arts today aren't associated with taking it easy.

Among the reasons for this misperception is something called the "mixed martial arts" (MMA). More a form of brutish brawling than a sophisticated mode of defense, MMA includes some techniques from traditional Asian fighting combined with Greek boxing and wrestling, Roman gladiator combat, and a freshly opened can of redneck barroom whup-ass.

Even those old movies from the '70s, where everybody was kung fu fighting, are uptight. All that running around, leaping, and screaming all over the place while beating the hell out of each other...it's all downright un-Dude. Couldn't they have just worked things out over oat sodas or rice Manchurians?

Other apparent disconnects between the Dude Way and the martial arts include:

- There are rules and strict regimens you have to follow in the martial arts, something the Dude would probably find exhausting.

- The Dude was a pacifist, was he not? Even when faced with castration, he never resorted to using a swift roundhouse kick to the head of the johnson-cutting nihilists he encountered. We're not dealing with Billy Jack or even Chuck Norris,[46] here.

Still, the Dude managed to abide through threatening situations in *The Big Lebowski* without spilling his beverage or ending up in a Folger's can with Donny. How was he able to prevail over all the rampant un-Dudeness around him, remain true to his pacifism, and still abide? Was it just luck, or was he practicing a secret martial art that we've uncovered called Dude-jitsu?

This is our concern.

Bruce Lee: A Brother Dudeist?

Even though he only weighed 135 pounds, when it comes to the martial arts (and life), Bruce Lee was not exactly a lightweight. In fact, the movies this Asian-American martial arts master made in the 1970s pretty much single-handedly created a new movie genre and popularized martial arts in America.

As swift and as lethal in his moves as a riled cobra, Lee was not a Chinaman who developed his prowess by working on the railroads. He practiced daily for six to ten hours, which really isn't a very lazy, Dude-like way of living. Nonetheless, when it came to his overall life philosophy, Lee had a lot in

---

46 Hallowed be his meme.

common with the Dude's basic ethos. In particular, there were three core tenets of Lee's philosophy that would have had the Dude raising his White Russian to him:

Authenticity

On staying true to oneself, Lee said:

> *Always be yourself, express yourself, have faith in yourself, do not go out and look for a successful personality and duplicate it.*

Never one for pretense, the Dude was always at ease with himself and had obviously spent much of his life avoiding the square community's ideas of success.

Going with the Flow

As high-strung as he appeared to be in his movies, Lee nonetheless believed that to be a true martial artist, you had to learn to relax and go with the flow:

> *Be like water making its way through cracks. Do not be assertive, but adjust to the object, and you shall find a way around or through it. If nothing within you stays rigid, outward things will disclose themselves.*

While the Dude had his moments when his thinking had become uptight, he always returned to the natural flow of things by flowing like Kahlúa over ice, or soaking in a bathtub full of water.

Simplicity

Bruce Lee also believed that martial arts should be simple. He knew that once a technique or a style became too complex, everything could go wrong:

> *To me, the extraordinary aspect of martial*
> *arts lies in its simplicity. The easy way is also the*
> *right way...*

These three aspects of the Dude's way of life and Lee's philosophy, which he called *Jeet Kune Do*, all add up to living simply, authentically, and in balance with the universe.

Another attribute the Dude and Lee have in common is they didn't get all uptight about living in the past.

Like many masters before him, ranging from the Shaolin monks to *The Karate Kid*'s Mr. Miyagi, Lee wasn't interested in maintaining 3,000 years of beautiful martial arts tradition. He knew that the true spirit of the martial arts is like Zen, which liberates you from the ego's false consciousness to flow right here and now with the cosmic groove.

In other words, practicing the martial arts can help you abide.

You Take the *Wu Wei*, and I'll Take the Dude Way

This sense of authentic balance that the martial arts engender is why many styles, including Lee's *Jeet Kune Do*, incorporate Taoism's ancient yin-yang icon into their emblems.

This symbol, representing harmony, unity, and balance, really ties the nature of the universe together and fits right in there with the abiding martial arts ethos. It represents more than just being at one with everything, though. On a deeper level, it embodies the vital creative energy that Taoism believes flows from, and permeates through, this cosmic oneness.

Many learned women and men throughout the centuries have disputed this energy's nomenclature: *qi, chi,* and whatnot. But when the whole concept abates, it really just comes down to "the rhythm, the driving power in all nature, the ordering principle behind all life," as world religions expert Huston Smith put it.

From this yin-yang principle emerges that important Taoist tenet that many martial artists share: *wu wei,* or "nondoing." Not to be confused with just being lazy, *wu wei* actually refers to the natural, spontaneous flow you experience when your life isn't all uptight and is lived instead from a relaxed yin-yang center.

"The person who embodies this condition," Smith blathered, "...acts without strain, persuades without argument, is eloquent without flourish, and achieves results without violence, coercion, or pressure."

Sounds a lot like abiding in the Dude Way, doesn't it? Parts, anyway.

Pacifism Is Not Something to Hide Behind

The Dude's definitely simpatico with the non-doing part of the martial arts. Because he wears professional martial arts shoes while doing something very similar to a *tai chi* move on his rug, he even seems to know something about these Asian disciplines.

Yet, the Dude was a pacifist too. Even with the whole *wu wei* thing going on, there's no getting around the "martial" in martial arts. Given the kick-ass mentality of today's MMA culture, pacifism and martial arts may seem contradictory. Considering the paradoxical yin-yang spirit of the martial arts, though, the two are in harmony and even promote a kick-back-and-abide ethos. It's like the founder of modern karate, Master Gichin Funakoshi, said:

> *To win one hundred victories in one hundred battles is not the highest skill. To subdue the enemy without fighting is the highest skill.*

As someone who was very skilled at being high, the Dude certainly took Funakoshi's maxim to heart. Even with the johnson-cutting nihilists, he wanted to end his predicament cheaply and pacify them without resorting to violence.

And that's what Dude-jitsu is all about.

The confrontation in the bowling alley parking lot between the nihilists and Walter, Donny, and the Dude is a good example of Dude-jitsu in action (or inaction). While the Dude just wants to go with the flow and hand over *ze money* to the nihilists, Walter resists and meets their threatened force with his own threat of force. Although the three bowling buddies get to keep their bullshit money as a result, the stress generated by Walter's aggressive way ultimately kills Donny.

Was it worth the cost?

Sure, Walter may have been in the dumps and lost a little money had he practiced some Dude-jitsu here, but a life would have also gone on, man. Though Walter may be a skilled and effective warrior, when it comes to the true spirit of martial arts, he is tragically out of his element.

The Art of Dude-Jitsu

That's why we are revealing here for the first time the secrets of Dude-jitsu. In a world filled with too many hee-roes dying face down in the muck, we believe the time is right to turn you on to this nonviolent practice (or non-practice).

The parking lot fight with the nihilists is an extreme example of applying Dude-jitsu in a dangerous situation. As the world's laziest martial art, this form of self-defense is usually nonphysical and a lot more passive than that. Some might even call Dude-jitsu passive-aggressive, which rather than being pejorative, accurately reflects its inherent yin-yang balance.

Like most martial arts, Dude-jitsu is rooted in keeping your mind limber and abiding in the *wu wei* flow represented by the yin-yang. Unlike other martial arts, this level of awareness isn't achieved through grueling physical workouts. In order to practice it, all you have to do is just take it easy, which is in harmony with the essence of a Japanese martial art called *jujitsu*.[47]

Jujitsu is considered a "soft" martial art, as opposed to "hard" forms that meet an opponent's force with hard, solid kicks and strikes. In *jujitsu*, which literally means "art of softness," you don't meet an opponent's physical force with your own force. Instead, like water, or *wu wei*, you flow with the opponent's force and use it against them to throw them off balance and flip them onto the floor before they even know what's happening.

---

47 Some say the proper nomenclature is actually *jujutsu*, but what are we now? Fucking participle rangers?

Dude-jitsu follows the same basic approach, only with one important difference: There's no physical harm intended. Instead, it uses an uptight person's *un-Dudeness* against them to throw them off balance mentally and then to flip them off verbally before they even know what's happening.

Fabulous stuff, man. But some may wonder if it qualifies as a martial art.

We believe it does because, like most martial arts, Dude-jitsu can trace its lineage a-way back into the mists of time to a feller by the name of Bodhidharma.

The Big Wu-bowski

Legend has it that Bodhidharma was a Buddhist monk from India in the 5th or 6th century who rambled off to China to teach monks in the Shaolin Buddhist monastery how to abide in practicing Zen.

The Shaolin monks must have been taking 'er a bit too easy at the monastery before he got there, however, because they weren't limber enough to keep up with Bodhidharma's meditative prowess.

So, to help keep the monks' minds and bodies agile enough for his form of abiding, Bodhidharma combined Zen meditation with a rigorous physical regimen of the fighting styles he had learned back in India. In the process, according to the story, this combination established what would become known as *kung fu*. As a result, Bodhidharma is credited with inspiring the bulk of martial arts forms (and a hit TV series from the 1970s) that evolved from Shaolin *kung fu*.

Although the influence of Bodhidharma's meditation/physical training is obvious in most martial arts styles, not many people are privy to how he also influenced the lazy and passive-aggressive art of Dude-jitsu. It can be found in the story [48] of Bodhidharma's visit to the emperor of China...a Chinaman named Wu. The Big Wu-bowski, as some have called the emperor, had invited Bodhidharma to his palace to discuss the tenets of Buddhism.

When he met the emperor, though, Bodhidharma found Wu verbally micturating all over the Dharma with self-important arrogance.

"No, not on the Dharma, man," Bodhidharma muttered.

After listening to the emperor go on about all the karmic merit he had achieved in his lifetime, the Zen dude told the Big Wu-bowski: "The Buddha spoke of no-mind, man, the non-attachment to life's illusions. Your karmic achievements will not stand. Your illusory merit will not stand, man."

The emperor was taken off balance by such insolence. "What in Buddha's holy name is Guatama's most fundamental teaching, then, you nitwit?" Wu demanded.

"Um, vast emptiness?" Bodhidharma offered. "Is that a...what sutra is that?"

The Big Wu-bowski was infuriated by Bodhidharma's casual indifference. "Who do you think you are?!" he yelled, slamming his fist down on the imperial throne.

"I have no idea, man...sir," Bodhidharma shrugged, reclining into his chair and sliding on a pair of jade sunglasses.

---

48 This version is a Dudeist translation of the traditional narrative. Other translators have their stories; we have ours.

Practicing Dude-Jitsu

In this classic example of Dude-jitsu, Bodhidharma went along with Emperor Wu's rigid un-Dudeness and used it against him, throwing him off balance before flipping him off with a verbal parry at the end. With Bodhidharma's limber mind, he remained centered in *wu wei* and was cool as clear water warshing over stones at the bottom of a mountain stream.

That's the key connection between Dude-jitsu and abiding—staying cool in the *wu wei* flow of things. The more stressed out your thinking is, the more uptight you become; the more uptight you become, the more shut off you are from the Dude Way's natural flow; the more uncentered you are from not abiding in this flow, the less able you are to flip off the unDudeness around you.

Throughout *The Big Lebowski*, the Dude effortlessly demonstrates his passive-aggressive mastery of the ancient practice of Dude-jitsu. When he encounters the un-Dude, his limberness of mind almost always allows him to sidestep and flip them off without losing his cool, deflecting their negative energy back onto them and letting their anger or uptightness burn them out.

Because practicing Dude-jitsu requires dude-ication to taking it easy, it may appear deceptively easy to do. If you're not flowing in the deep currents of the Dude Way *wu wei* when you deal with the un-Dude, it's amazing how quickly you'll find yourself stuck face down in the muck of their un-Dudeness. Aside from following a strict drug regimen, there are ways you can keep your mind limber enough to prevent that from happening. You *do* want to know.

First, regularly incorporate into your daily life the abiding principles of dudeitation and Dudeist yoga outlined in this guide. As with everything else in life, all of these practices are really just different names for different aspects of the same essential yin-yang thing going on. The more these practices become an integral part of your routine, the more your consciousness will loosen up and float along with the Dude Way's flow.

As your mind becomes more like water—or perhaps more like Kahlúa—you'll develop a level of mindfulness that will enable you to keep going with the flow even when confronted with the un-Dude.

The Dude's No Mind

This sensibility is an important part of practicing the martial arts as well as abiding in the Dude Way. There is a Japanese Zen expression that means "mind of no mind." It basically refers to when your mind is free of all ego concerns and you are totally at ease in the current moment. In Japanese, it's called *mushin no shin*.

In English, we Dudeists refer to it as *not givin' a shit*.

Once you have attained this frameless frame of reference, grasshopper, you, too, will be a Dude-jitsu master. Ancient Chinese secret? Far from it.

For more study into the ancient art of Dude-jitsu, please visitdudeism.com/dudejitsu.

SOME KIND OF YOGA

A Natural, Zesty Exercise

If you squint a little, the Dude looks like a wise old Asian sage: robe, sandals, long hair, and a goatee. The robe may be polyester (we own an exact replica), the sandals plastic (got those too), and the goatee a few shades paler than you'd find in China, but perhaps down deep he carries the soul of Lao Tzu with him. Or at least, a low-rent Alan Watts.

Of course, this is no accident: Anyone who had an active role in the '60s cultural revolution should be at least leisurely familiar with a variety of Eastern philosophies and practices. The Dude manages to mix a little West into his East, however. He practices a bit of *tai chi*, but with a White Russian in one hand; he has a book of Japanese cooking on his coffee table next to In-n-Out Burger wrappers; he performs a bit of what might be *chi gong* (a Chinese energy meditation) while listening to bowling and Bob Dylan; he responds with "What is that, some kind of Eastern thing?" when confronted with an obscure old Western cowboy aphorism; and finally, just after engaging in coitus with Maude he sees her clutching her knees to her chin and inquires, "What is that, some kind of yoga?" At no point in the movie does he appear an expert Orientalist, but he clearly digs a lot of the Asian style, even if he's hardly orthodox in his approach to these all-too-transcendental traditions.

Ever since the '60s, Asian spirituality has become integrated in Western culture—parts anyway. Though it may not pray in Peoria, "Eastern things" are a big part of the self-help and new-age corpus—that strange and seemingly incompatible meeting point where metaphysics and merchandising intermingle.

Echoing the Dude's query to Maude, one of the Asian traditions that has most captured the imagination of the

West is known as *yoga*. If we understand it *incorrectly*, yoga is a series of physical exercises designed to give you the biceps of Madonna, the sexual stamina of Sting, and the earning potential of Deepak Chopra. The truth is, though, yoga can be all those things. Physical-exercise yoga is called *hatha yoga*, sexual/sensual yoga is called *tantra yoga*, and Chopra's shrewd rebranding of ancient ideas is called *scamdya yoga*. Ha ha, just kidding. Uh, *Oprah yoga*? Well, dude, we just don't know. We'll have to check with our accountant. But yoga is also much more than this.

There are seemingly infinite varieties of yoga, all seen as paths toward the same central enlightenment. This is how Hinduism is able to be both polytheistic and monotheistic at the same time—they say, "Truth is one, though the sages speak of it by many names." Thus, Maude's weird wriggling on the bed designed to make the Dude's seed travel less languidly could be called a form of yoga, so long as she's in the right frame of mind when she performs it. The common denominator linking all forms of yoga is *mindfulness*; that is, we should be highly aware of whatever it is we're doing, in the moment, with the flow, facing the situation full on, however pleasant or painful it may be.

It's easy to accuse the Dude of being anything but mindful in his actions. Stoned half of the time, buzzed the other, and more or less baffled during the entire stretch of the movie, he hardly appears the paragon of focused awareness that the Yogic sages would prescribe for enlightened living. And yet, by the time the film is over, we realize that he is the only one who is actually processing the world in a way that accords with determined (if drowsy) intellectual inquiry.

Though the Coens' intention may have been to place the most ill-prepared candidate in the role of film noir sleuth, it is ironic but appropriate that he turns out to be the man for his time and place. Why? Because he's the only character who fucking listens occasionally (often, actually) and learns something. With no preconceptions and a friendly, open, and painfully honest approach, the Dude exhibits the child-like nature that most sages prescribe as a first step to students of earnest inquiry.

We might say that the Dude is a disciple of the *jnana yoga* tradition. *Jnana yoga* is a process of finding the fundamental truth of reality via a process of *neti neti*, or negation—it is not this, it is not that. Thus the Dude keeps his mind open and entertains all possibilities, until at last through a process of elimination he finds what he is looking for. All the other characters have already made their minds up about things and so can never begin the process of "enlightening up." The Dude might resist a bit at times, especially when dealing with his intellectual bully buddy Walter, but on the whole, he's willing to entertain anything.

Though the principles underlying the Yogic tradition existed long before, it was the sage Patanjali who codified it into the "eight-limbed" path. Mark it eight, Dude. One of those eight "limbs" is called asanas and refers to the physical type of yoga favored by Westerners, probably because of all the yogic paths, it alone is useful for making one's ass look more desirable. What is surprising is that if you translate asana into English it literally means "seat." So, it's about using your ass for what it is most evidently designed for—not to attract mates, but to sit upon.

Yoga asanas were created and codified by Hindu sages not for physical fitness, but for spiritual fitness; because long periods of meditation were central to the mystic tradition, it was important that the body be able to sit for long periods while the person endeavors to purify and expand the contents of the mind. In fact, some scholars argue that the gymnastic aspect to Indian Yoga appeared as late as the 19th or 20th century! Thus, all this "posing" that's so popular with pop stars seems to be rather the opposite of the original intention. And conversely, the Dude's languid laying about while mellowing his mind appears to resurrect the lost traditions of Patanjali and the sages of ancient Asia.

We might ask, as we watch the Dude laze about with eyes half open: "What is that, some kind of yoga?" Three thousand years of booty-full tradition—you're goddamn right he's lounging in the past. Never mind circus tricks like handstands and lotus positions; it is the Dude's positions of extreme relaxation that deserve our emulation.

With this in mind, we identify some of the Dude's signature yoga postures, and discuss how best to perform them for maximum Dudelightenment potential.

The Dudeist Some Kind of Yoga Poses (Asanas)

Spacing Out Asana

When we first meet the Dude, we see him shuffle through the aisles at Ralphs supermarket, then stop and sniff a carton of half-and-half. Not only is the Dude profoundly relaxed, but he is staring into the distance for an unusually long time for someone who is flagrantly breaking a supermarket rule with evidence in hand. Thus, we see in Spacing Out Asana that we can be in a potentially stressful situation (standing, vulnerable) while still remaining comfortable, meditative, and utterly unworried. It's all about striking the perfect balance. Neither here nor there.

Tips: The key to this posture is the pushing forward of the hips, as this makes use of the back and leg muscles unnecessary for balance. Also, the feet should be spread wide, despite the fact that it might confer the appearance of an inelegant duck. And finally, the elbows should be resting against the body for maximum stability and relaxation of the arms. Accoutrements like a beverage or a joint will likewise be easily held aloft for long periods in this position.

Toilet Seat Asana

After the thugs give him a hard time and piss on his rug, the Dude is seen sitting on the toilet, striving to calm himself down. The toilet is one of the finest places upon which we can take refuge from the world. Especially for those of us who live in cities, the bathroom is the one place we can be sure to acquire some privacy and achieve peace of mind. The next time you go into your bathroom or even a public toilet stall, make sure to take an extra minute to relax and find the still center within.

Tips: Voiding the bowels and the bladder can be perceived as a metaphor for letting go of other forms of shit that might accumulate inside you over the course of a day. Try to let go of the figurative shit as you let go of the literal shit.

Then new shit can come to light, instead of darkness warshing over like a black steer's tookus.[49]

Bowling Argument Asana

While arguing with Walter over what to do about the rug, the Dude almost loses his cool until he performs the bowler's back stretch. It is a difficult pose, but one that can be profoundly humbling as well. Resembling the "trust exercises" of corporate retreats, the Dude bends backward and surrenders to gravity, but then catches himself and stands back up again. This particular asana can't be performed too often in a short time period, but is a useful tool when we are particularly strung out and need to do something drastic to calm down. Note that as he launches into the pose, he stops yelling at Walter and says instead, "That's fucking interesting." Bowling Argument Asana is a great way to resolve conflict and keep our minds limber.

Tips: Spread your legs wide and don't bend back too much or you might pull a muscle or fall over. Do this a maximum of five times at first. Don't worry if your belly or underwear[50] shows while performing this asana—remember, it is about inculcating humility, so looking silly is actually an important aspect of the pose.

---

49 Mystical novelist and spiritual teacher Carlos Castaneda was likely a big believer in Toilet Seat Asana. He is reported to have said, "If one gets 'silent' enough on the *bowl*, a crack in the world opens up."

50 In fact, the part of the belly and underwear the Dude shows in this scene is an important Dudeist energy center— the "undies chakra." (See "Thankie," page 234, for more about this.)

The Take It Easy Chair Asana

When being berated by the elder Lebowski, the Dude adopts an increasingly relaxed position, sinking down ever lower and slouchier in the chair opposite the old man's imposing wooden desk. It is not a pose of surrender or submission; rather it is a position of the highest confidence. When confronted by aggression that will not stand, it is better to slouch languidly in response than to try to match it with an equally aggressive attitude. He who considers himself to be acting with integrity and enlightenment need not engage in a provocative display. Looking comfortable while others try to make you uncomfortable not only is the best way to defuse their attack, but also helps you to feel calm and invulnerable. Think of the unconcerned aspect of Peter, the protagonist in the movie *Office Space*. His boss' criticisms can have no effect when they are ignored entirely. Note that the Dude employs the same asana when dealing with Jackie Treehorn and the Malibu police chief.

Tips: Whenever you're seated in a chair, find the most comfortable posture you can. This may vary from chair to chair, so it is good to practice this pose in many different styles of chair. Go to a furniture store and try out all the different types they have on display. When a salesman comes over to ask what you want to buy, tell him or her that you are just "practicing." They will probably leave you alone after that. Even in chairs or sofas you may own, try to find new and more relaxing positions you haven't tried before. Look at all the various poses the Dude employs throughout the film in the seated position for inspiration. You'd be surprised how many different ways he positions his body while seated—it borders on an art form. Then again, remember that asana means "seated." It's easy to forget how creative the very act of sitting still can be.

The Peaceful Warrior Asana

One of the most famous poses in popular yoga is called "the warrior pose." As you might have guessed, it is very linear and aggressive. The Dude performs a similar, if tangled, version of this while standing on his rug with a White Russian in hand. Though it resembles a *tai chi* pose, we know of no official *tai chi* pose that incorporates a beverage.

Tips: In fact, this pose is very similar to a famous statue of one of the most beloved Hindu gods, Shiva. Shiva is the "destroyer" god. And though an alcoholic beverage may be incorporated in the pose, it is probably better not to get too "destroyed"—otherwise you're likely to fall over and spill your White Russian on the rug.

Rugasana

Though popular yoga includes plenty of wildly acrobatic poses—some that make Maude flying in her harness look positively pedestrian—it also has some very easy and relaxing ones as well. Shavasana, or "corpse pose" is surely the coziest one of all—you lay on your back on the floor quiet and still as a corpse. The Dude, of course, is a master of this pose. He performs his own modified version as he lies on the rug and listens to recordings of old bowling tournaments.

Though the idea may seem humorous to the novice Dudeist Yogi, the Dude is in fact engaging in a serious form of preparation for his upcoming tournament, arguably more powerful than the bowling practice itself. It's been shown repeatedly in scientific studies that taking time to imagine yourself performing an act will aid you in the skillful and graceful execution of that act, far more so than will merely practicing the act in real-world conditions. Sounds amazing, we know, but that's what the boys down at the lab tell us.

At least in part, one imagines that the Dude so gracefully skates through life due to the fact that he's such an Olympic-class daydreamer, a gold-medal relaxer. So the next time you have a problem or a challenge to face, imagine yourself making it to the finals before even putting on your bowling shoes.

Tips: Note that the Dude also moves his hands about as he listens—this is ostensibly to help aid the flow of *Chill* (the Dudeist term for Chinese *chi*, or spiritual energy). You don't officially need a rug to perform rugasana—but you will probably find it easier to take it easy if you're lying on something soft.

Fuggedaboudit Asana

When the Dude sits in the back of Maude's limo, in limbo between two tragedies (losing a million dollars, being presented with the ransom toe), he enjoys a momentary spell of elation. Tony the limo driver tells him "fuggedaboudit," and the Dude adds, "Can't be worried about that shit! Life goes on, man!" But the words he speaks are only a part of the position. Note that he is sitting in what would generally be considered a rather gauche, inelegant pose—with his package exposed for all the world (or, at least, Tony) to see.

We spend so much time hiding our genitals from the world, that it can be liberating to stick them out and say "Fuck it" to convention. Practice sitting exactly as he does, with one foot up, the other dangling and your beaver or johnson unprotected and vulnerable. Please, feel free to inspect them!

Tips: This doesn't have to be performed in public to be effective. We can't be held responsible for any injury that may occur while performing Fuggedaboudit asana. Use your own best judgment. For extra power, say the lines quoted above as you perform the pose, incorporating the hand gesture elements of "The Dude Abides Asana" as outlined below.

Dead in the Water Asana

There are a lot of references to liquids in *The Big Lebowski*—from the Dude buying a carton of half-and-half to Woo peeing on the rug to a flurry of White Russians and oat sodas. There are also quotes like "Careful man, there's a beverage here" and "You guys are dead in the water," scenes of the Dude in the bath with an amphibious rodent, crocodile tears at which we are meant to be surprised, and ultimately, the bosom of the Pacific Ocean. It's no wonder, of course, as Taoism makes water its central metaphor, and the Dude is a modern Taoist master. How does he go with the flow? By imitating water. Considering the fact that our bodies are made up of 70 percent of the stuff, this shouldn't be so hard to do. Careful, man—there's a beverage here!

The easiest way to practice imitating water is to spend a lot of time in it. Some theories contend that human beings spent most of their evolutionary history hanging out near large bodies of water and this is why we like swimming and bathing so much.[51] Thus, lying back and relaxing in a tub or a pool or a lake is an easy and logical asana to undertake, provided one has access. For those who don't, the experience can be simulated by laying back on an inflatable air mattress while soaking one's feet in a shallow pail of warm water. Then go ahead and meditate. But be careful! Remember what happened to that guy in the 1980 movie *Altered States*. Dead in the Water Asana can be very transformative.

Tips: Bath salts can help enhance the experience by more closely simulating the saltwater lake that ancient humans were meant to have hung out in (not to mention, the saltwater all of us spent our first nine months hanging out in). Whale sounds, candles, and a bit of mind-limbering elixir can also help you get into the right frame of restfulness. Make sure to lock your door securely to prevent nihilists from breaking in and spoiling the mood.

The Barasana

We can't spend all our time holed up in our private residences. When out on the town you might find yourself in a stressful situation, just as the Dude does when he's trying to deal with the threats of the nihilists and Walter doesn't have the patience or wisdom to help him "buck up." In that

---

51 Though Elaine Morgan's "Aquatic Ape Hypothesis" (which states that humans are radically adapted to living in aquatic environments) has been controversial, even mainstream theorists believe that humans are unusually predisposed among primates to make use of aquatic environments. It's possible that the earliest human settlements sprung up alongside a huge inland lake in Ethiopia. The lake would have provided not only abundant food, but also protection from big cats, their most worthy fucking adversary.

case, employing a sturdy counter to slouch against while we try to collect our thoughts can make all the difference. At the very least, it can implore kind-hearted Strangers to offer condolences. In fact, that's probably why bars were designed in the first place—to provide comfort, solace, and sympathy to those looking to temporarily bathe their sorrows.

Tips: Practice making a powerful pyramid shape with your elbows resting on the counter and supporting your head. Breathe slowly in and out as you focus on the cocktail or bowl of peanuts in front of you. Repeat to yourself: "Sometimes you eat the bar, and sometimes the bar, well, he eats you."

Gutterballet Asana

When darkness truly warshes over and you have nowhere else to go, Gutterballet Asana is just the ticket. Gutterballet Asana is performed by getting up off of the floor (or the coffee table) and dancing like a total fucking amateur. It may be hard to accomplish this in public with so many people laughing and pointing at you, so at first, you're better off doing this in the privacy of your bungalow. Put on some music you find particularly lively and dance like the Dude does in the second dream sequence. Or any way that feels good. After a few minutes, you'll be giggling like the Auto Circus cop after the Dude asks him if he's got any leads. Laughable, man!

Tips: If you can summon the courage, Gutterballet Asana is even more fun when performed with other like-minded Dudeists. A few White Russians can help ease you into it and remove the social awkwardness associated with... uh...social awkwardness. Gutterballet Asana can help fix the broken cable that is keeping your life full of static. The important thing is expressly not to look cool. Even if you are a fine dancer, you should try to dance in a way that would suggest that you're not. This isn't the guy who built the Soul Train, here. This is an easy way to step on your sadness, und skvish it.

Upward Lazing Dude

How often do we notice ceilings? At Jackie Treehorn's "unspoiled pad" the Dude adopts an impressive series of comfortable slouches, one especially noteworthy for the lazy upward gaze that the Dude perpetrates. You don't see people sit like that very often. With belly hanging out and chin up, the Dude comes across as a blissful Buddha, belly up to the great beyond. Sitting like that is equivalent to a sort of "surrender" to the heavens—an embracing of the immense unknown, a bit like falling upward.

Tips: Treehorn's couches were specially built for deep angles of recline. You might have to use some pillows to support your back to help you comfortably lean back that far. The back is fragile, man. Very fragile. It also ties all the nerves together. When performing some kind of yoga, make sure to keep your mind lumbar.

Deeply Casual Asana

The Big Lebowski contains perhaps one of the most extraordinary examples of *slackrobatics* ever recorded on film. When Treehorn momentarily steps out of the room, the Dude pads over to see what he wrote on his notepad. But then, when he hears Jackie coming back, he rushes back to the couch and instantly slides into a fully relaxed reclining position. It is so hilariously seamless, so utterly graceful, that we can only presume the Dude has practiced for years to instantly relax on command. Slackomatic!

To learn this very useful and extraordinary technique, just stand up next to a couch or soft chair and drop yourself into the same relaxed pose as the Dude. Do this over and over until it can be performed effortlessly. You'll find that this will train you to relax in all sorts of other types of situations, and that you'll be able to escape tension with the same skill and facility as the master himself.

Tips: Exaggerate the tension as you stand, balling your fists and clenching your jaw. That way, when you finish lowering yourself onto the couch, the difference between the two states will be all the greater. Make sure to take care when lying backward—you don't want to hurt yourself. Remember that the Dude is a trained professional. Note as well that you can perform variants of this asana while seated—just tense your body and face, and then release everything. Repeat over and over until you achieve some mastery and can summon relaxation at will. That'll get the stress to stop talking!

Abideasana

At least three times in the film, the Dude performs a subtle but powerful Dudeist yoga technique designed to rid the body of nervous energy. The pose consists of letting the hands fly up to the sides like the upstroke of a bird flapping its wings. This is called Abideasana because it helps us to maintain an abiding approach to the ups and downs, strikes and gutters in our lives.

The first time we see it is in the limo with Tony, when the Dude says, "Can't be worried about that shit. Life goes on." Immediately afterward, in the limo with Lebowski and Brandt, the Dude performs a string of them, as if deflecting a steady stream of arrows. Finally, at the very end, when the Stranger says, "Take it easy, Dude. I know that you will," the Dude throws up his hands in the same way, as if conducting the end of an orchestral movement and says, "Yeah, well, you know, the Dude abides." It is a signature move that essentially says "Oh well" or "Hey ho" to all the unexpected setbacks that undermine our attempts to take it easy. By performing this gesture over and over, we can help introduce an easy way to brush off the bummers that would otherwise pull us down in the dumps.

If you master all of these poses and you'd like to find an excellent and fun way to feed the monkey, why not start your own Some-Kind-of-Yoga studio? Why should the sweaty acrobats have all the fun?

For more discussion or to suggest poses, please visit: dudeism.com/yoga.

THANKIE

The Power of Dudeiversal Energy

By Rev. Andrea Favro

Rev. Andrea Favro, the Dudeship of Italy, is a longtime contributor to the Dudespaper, *and he's helped introduce many spiritual ideas to our rug-based religion. He maintains and edits dudeismo.org, the popular Italian portal for Dudeism, from his pad in Northern Italy. His catchphrase is* Abideamo!

Learn the ancient art of Thankie and you'll be thankful. And who knows, you might even be able one day to call the Stranger compeer and to become one of the Immortal Dudes who wander around the earth helping other Dudes to deal with the durned human comedy.

Before telling you about this ancient Eastern art, I need to talk a little about *yin*, *yang*, and *chi*. I know these are touched on in other parts of this book so I hope it won't be exhausting, but we need the right frame of reference here. According to our Taoist compeers, everything that exists is subject to the interaction of two opposing forces: the yin and the yang. Their movement or alternation creates *chi* or *ki*, the living energy that permeates everything that exists in infinite ways and at infinite degrees. Yeah, it's pretty far-out, if we understand it correctly.

As you know, everything yin has a part of yang, and everything yang has a part of yin. Just like Walter has a bit of Dudeness in his heart and the Dude also displays a bit of the Walterish from time to time. Yin and yang actually are not opposing forces, rather they border, define, and meld into each other in the same way that ups and downs, strikes and gutters, Dude and un-Dude, Pacific ocean and beach community, and half-and-half could not exist without each other. They transform themselves continuously into their opposite, and in this way create *chi*. This continuous transformation is needed for the health of living systems—if something is

totally yin, you end up with immobility. And if something is completely yang, you have burnout, or explosion, or nihilists torching your fucking car.

Now the concept of *chi*, or the "universal living energy"—that's something that really made a lot of sense to our Chinese compeers. But it's not just some kind of Chinese thing—it was also known as *pneuma* in ancient Greece and Rome, as *prana* in India, and as *ki* in Japan. Many arts have been developed to access this universal infinite energy, or force, to use it to heal and to deal better with life itself. Techniques like *chi gong*, *tai chi*, *aiki*, and *pranayama* are all well known these days. However, it seems that the energy technique that seems to pull the most water in the West lately is called *Reiki* (pronounced rayee-key).

Let me tell you a couple of things about Reiki: Much like other arts, it began as a very simple technique to heal oneself and others. Today it's become a much more business-oriented thing. Mr. Usui, the Japanese founder, practiced it for free or for a small fee. Today you usually have to pay thousands of dollars for a two-day class to get a piece of paper stating that you are a Master of Reiki. Someone's trying to scam everyone here, man. The goal of Reiki as Usui intended it was to be the simplest possible way to reconnect with nature and to access the universal life energy to increase health and live better. Usui would never have dreamed of taking your bullshit money.

Reiki (the original, uncompromised first draft) was a method to teach you to be your own healer. Think of the Stranger: He doesn't show the Dude how cool he is or how to be cool; he just asks the right questions, listens to the answers, and gives the right and needed input to help the Dude pull himself out of the dumps. Some people think the Stranger is just a part of the Dude's imagination. Far out. But that's a good way to express how our Dudeist version of Reiki—called *Thankie*—works. Basically, we can be our own "smarter feller than ourselves."

There are many techniques to increase or use *chi* in our daily life, but most of them are either difficult to learn or just too complicated for a common Dude who just wants to feel better without having to train for hours every day. *Thankie* uses two simple things: your breath and a bit of imagination. Actually, imagination is needed during the first part of your practice; it will be replaced afterward by knowledge and feeling, but at the beginning, imagining is enough.

While at the beginning we'll need to practice it and to imagine a little of what's going on inside and around us, devoting time to practicing *Thankie* will become second nature, just like learning to use a bike or a car. Make it to practice, dudes, and you'll make it to the finals every day without feeling like the good universe gypped you.

Okay then, let's dig the style of *Thankie*:

1. Belly Handles

To employ the full power of *Thankie* we must relearn to breathe naturally. It's actually easier than it seems. Breathing naturally using our belly is an ability we all possess, but something most of us have forgotten in this age of uptight thinking.

Instructions: Lie down on your sofa; put one hand on your chest and the other on your belly, and look at how they move when you breathe. If you are like most human beings, the only hand that moves is the one on your chest, or that's the one that moves first. Natural breathing, or belly breathing, instead requires you to breathe using your belly so that when you breathe in, your belly extends, and when you breathe out, your belly contracts. This will also help you to strengthen your belly muscles and maybe reduce your beer belly. If you do it correctly, the hand on your belly will move first now. To get a couple of examples, look at how your baby, or cat, or dog breathes and do the same. As a matter of fact, when we are infants we all breathe this way.

2. Go With the Yin and Yang Flow

When we breathe in, we visualize yin energy coming in from the sky through the top of our heads down through our whole body passing through our *undies chakra*.[52] This is two or three inches down from your belly button, usually where the elastic waistband on your underwear sits. From there, imagine it passing through your feet and on into the earth. When we breathe out, imagine yang energy going in the opposite direc-

---

52 According to Indian Ayurvedic medicine, chakras are energy centers in our bodies. The Chinese and the Indians disagree on how many there are and where they are located, but they all agree on the existence and relative importance of the *undies chakra*, although they don't call it that. If you're not into that whole brevity thing, you can also refer to the head as the "strands in Duder's head chakra" and the feet the "fucking toes chakra."

tion: from the earth, through us and up to the sky. "From my toes up to my ears," as Bob Dylan sings in "The Man in Me." Dylan, of course, is a *Thankie* master.

3. Making It to Practice

Every morning, lie down on your sofa and practice for 20 breaths in the manner described above. Pause for a second or two between each breath. And always use your belly as the engine of your respiration, not your chest. If you like, you can then repeat the twenty breaths at midday and in the evening to get faster results. Soon, breathing this way will become automatic.

4. Further Uses of Thankie

The Lake of Dudeness

The *undies chakra* is a very powerful energy center. As you practice *Thankie*, you'll become aware of your *undies chakra* to the point where you will actually be able to "see" it. When you are feeling unwell, imagine waves of harmony starting from your *undies chakra* and spreading calm and coolness everywhere, like waves spreading around a cell phone thrown into a lake.

Shoosh!

At times it can happen that one's mind isn't as limber as it should be. Too many strands in ol' Duder's head. In that case, the Chinese would say there's not too many strands, but too much heat in ol' Duder's head. These are times when imagining the flow of cool yin going down to the earth can become useful to empty our mind and make it limber once again. The opposite is also true: When our minds are too limber, imagining the upward flow of hot yang can help us think in a more focused way. If you are into that whole mantra thing, it can be pretty useful to think the word "shoosh" to symbolize the flow of yin or yang moving down or up. "Shoosh" and your mind gets limber. "Shoosh" and it snaps to attention. *Shoosh*. You won't lose your train of thought or ramble so much again.

Practicing *Thankie* on Others

While a big part of Reiki is about "laying hands" on (or near, actually) other people to heal their sicknesses, many learned men (even graduates of two-day Master of Reiki courses) have disputed this. When it comes to the transfer of *chi* from one person to another, well, dude, we just don't know. But it couldn't hurt, and concentrating on the concerns of folks in need can be profoundly pleasant for all interested parties. We invite you to sign up and send free Dudeiversal energy to anyone who needs it via our site: dudeism.com/thankie. Just don't try and scam anyone here, man.

Even if you don't want to practice *Thankie* on others, just practicing it on yourself can help make the world a better place. When you use *Thankie* to calm yourself down and strengthen your own spirits, you'll be able to spread waves of relaxation, coolness, and calm all around, wherever you go. You can influence others' lives just by being Dudely—abiding by example. And that's cool, that's cool.

That's it! Now you are a *Thankie* Master and no longer a Stranger to the Dudeiversal energy of the Universe. *Shoosh*.

For your free online *Thankie* Master certificate, just visit: dudeism.com/thankie.

FUNGIN' SHWAY

The Dudeist Science of Really Tying Your Room Together

It's perhaps odd that a film that is so concerned with "what makes a man" also features home decorating so prominently in its story. Traditionally, a well-furnished home has been seen as something requiring a "woman's touch." Well, *The Big Lebowski* is also about exploding gender stereotypes, so maybe that's why the Dude (and other fellows in the film) are so concerned with tying the room together, keeping their pads totally unspoiled, displaying various awards and commendations, or at least just fixing the cable.

Certainly, the Coen Brothers have always paid close attention to set design—from the transcendent trailer-park chic of *Raising Arizona* to the metaphysical circles and lines of *The Hudsucker Proxy* to the peeling wallpaper and portentous wall-hangings of *Barton Fink*, the backgrounds of their stories are nearly as important as their foregrounds. This is another reason why wide angles play so prominently in their films: to make us privy to more information, man. And to provide deeper "frames of reference." It's something we often forget in our own lives: Our environment helps define who we are. It shapes our moods, influences our attitudes. This is an eternal truth not lost on the Dude. After all, all he ever wanted was his rug back. Not greedy. It not only tied the room together, but it formed an integral part of his consciousness. Lotta strands in ol' Duder's head, and on his floor.

The Chinese art of *feng shui* (pronounced "fung shway") is an ancient quasimystical system intended to promote greater harmony of living via the arrangement of buildings, doorways, furniture, and other aspects of our environment. Though the beliefs of many *feng shui* practitioners are based on creepy superstitions, there are some practical aspects that can help even the most rational thinking Dudes out there. That's what our Dudeist art and science of *Fungin' Shway* (rhymes with Fuckin' A) is all about.

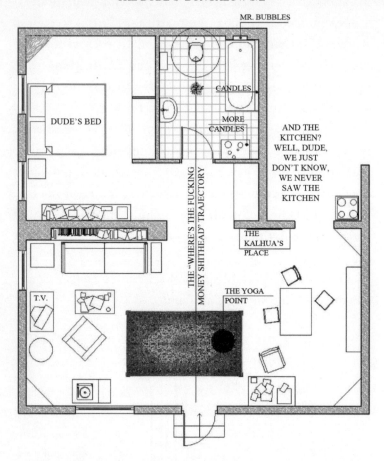

To set the stage, above is a blueprint of the Dude's home. It was designed by The Arch Dude of Chile, Andrea Maria Atenas.[53] She is a good draftswoman and thurrah.

Keeping both this blueprint and scenes from the film in mind, here are some important elements that can help provide your private residence with a Dude's touch:

---

53 Andrea is also part of "The Maude Squad." (See "Subjects Like Women," page 156.)

The John

The Throne

When the Dude leaves the Lebowski mansion, Brandt tells him to come back and visit some time. The Dude replies, "Sure, if I'm in the neighborhood, need to use the john." It could be taken as a sarcastic remark, but it also could identify the Dude's inverted hierarchy of priorities. Whereas the old Lebowski might favor his office or the so-called "Great Room" where he ruminates over the meaning of manhood, the Dude most likely esteems his commodious commode above all else. What is a mansion after all, but a giant support system for a bathroom? When it comes down to it, homes are there to help us protect our bodies and allow us a safe place to administer to the ablutions of both the body and the soul. Often under-appreciated, the bathroom is surely the most important place in the house. Treat it as the nave of your temple, both house and body—the holy of the *holeys*, as it were.

The Bath Cave

Decades ago, it was more common for people to take baths than showers. Now no one has the time for a proper long, hot bath with candles and whale sounds. But a bathtub turns the room into a womb, especially with the aforementioned accoutrements. If you're lucky enough to have a tub in your house, then by all means use it more often. A daily bath is the easiest and most powerful way to relax. Witness the rise of the spa industry, where you pay people a load of bones or clams or what-have-you just to take a glorified version of a bath, but with all sorts of overpriced goops and plinky plinky music in the background. Fungin' Shway is here to burst that bubble, man, with ah, you know, Mr. Bubble. And also: cheap candles, "The Song of the Whale," and a bit of premium dope. All that beats chocolate rubs and aromatherapy oil hands down (and toes up!). It is far more modestly priced as well.

Note that according to Dudevolutionary theory, early humans spent a lot of time hanging out in the water. Thus, baths are a way not only to tie the womb together, but to feed the monkey mind as well. (See "Some Kind of Yoga," page 218.)

The Rug

Usually "being grounded" is something that people esteem because it means that you're not a dreamer. This is not what it means in Dudeism, of course. Dudeism loves dreaming of all sorts—daydreams, dreams enjoyed while sleeping in, acid flashbacks, wild dream sequences involving crazed dancers and flying carpets, and so on. In Dudeism, "being grounded" has a different meaning. It means that you have a close relationship with the earth. Note that the Dude spends a lot of time there: meditating while lying on his rug, knocked down by the police chief of Malibu, floating along the bowling lanes in his dream, doing *tai chi*, etc. He doesn't live on a hill like Lebowski or Treehorn, or in a high-rise loft like Maude. As that old blues tune puts it, the Dude is "almost level with the ground," but in a good way. And that's cool, man, that's cool, that's cool. (Literally—heat rises.) A good rug can help us retain balance, by reminding us that what is low can help make us high as well.

The Bar

You don't have to be a drinker to be a practicing Dudeist. The Dude's tiki bar is just his take on what others might call a "shrine." His Kahlúa, vodka, half-and-half, ice bucket, and glasses are just his own personal sacraments. Perhaps in this discussion of Dudeist *feng shui*, it's a bit ironic that a poster of Richard Nixon hovers over his shrine—it was after Nixon's visit to China in 1972 that *feng shui* became popularized in the United States. Despite being a real reactionary, Nixon helped introduce Asian philosophy and culture to the U.S., just as hipper Dudes like Alan Watts and Ram Dass did in the 1960s. But of course Fungin' Shway is far more ironic and less serious than Nixon, Mao, and the rigid and superstitious nature of the original, uncompromised *feng shui*. Thus, our "shrine" is best conceived as fanciful and fun-loving. Dudeism is a religion that esteems humor and levity above all, so our shrine or bar or altar or whatever you call it should be a place that inspires us to laugh and feel all warm inside. Clearly hanging a poster of Nixon bowling is just Jeffrey being fatuous. And when practiced with affection and humility, fatuousness can be far-out indeed.

Sofa, So Good

Perhaps the most important piece of furniture one can ever invest in is a good sofa. In the pantheon of home furnishings, it is big daddy Zeus, the all-sitting, all-enveloping master of all it *sofays*. A good couch is all things to the broad masses of asses: a bed, a chair, a lounge, a desk, a storage space, a place to collect loose change, a source of fort-making materials (for

Little Lebowskis), a theater, a bordello, a dinette set, and so on. Though we only see the Dude use his to entertain guests (the police), we can easily imagine that he uses it for all of his daily business. Note how comfortable the Dude is on Jackie Treehorn's banquette sofa—it fits him like a papal throne.

Though the Dude also has a very comfortable-looking reclining chair, the detectives down at the Church of the Latter-Day Dude lab recommend the fabulous sectional sofa instead. It's a better value, more versatile, and doesn't have any troublesome moving parts.

Bedrock and Roll

Most people spend a third of their lives in bed—Dudeists often considerably more. Thus, ensuring that our bed is properly outfitted is crucial to the well-being of the principled Dudeist priest. What's more, it's not only a place for sleeping, but also for "fun and games" as Maude calls it—or rather, doesn't.

There are several things to note about the Dude's bed. First of all, his head is right next to a window. Given that he enjoys smoking dope while in bed, it makes sense, otherwise the whole area would be dark with thick resin. But aside from ventilating marijuana fumes, a good supply of oxygen is important to a good sleep. Unless you live in a very cold climate, keeping the window open a crack has been shown to be amenable to the quality of one's slumber.

Secondly, there are several books in the Dude's bedroom. We can assume that he reads before going to sleep. Now, not only is it important to enjoy regular reading to keep the mind limber, but reading before bed has been shown to be a powerful sedative and good for the quality of one's dreamtime. Twenty minutes to a half an hour of reading before dropping off is a cheap and easy way to enhance sleep and mental health. Plus, it turns you into a smarter feller than yourself.

Tying Things Up

This is just a brief overview of what we hope will become at least as sophisticated a science as the thousands-years-old Chinese tradition of *feng shui*. We encourage people to contact us with Fungin' Shway home furnishing suggestions at our website (dudeism.com/shway). Help us tie the whole world together, man. Our lives are in your floor plans.

DUDE ECONOMICS

by Rev. Joshua Max

Our pal and compeer Rev. Joshua Max writes regularly for Forbes Magazine (among others) and plays a mean (in a good way) guitar. We asked him to weigh in on the Dude's attitude toward money. Here's his brief take on Dudeism and the feeding of the monkey.

Dudeists may stress about a few life challenges, but money isn't one of them.

You write a check for 69 cents to pay for a quart of milk without a second thought—in fact, you do a little boogie on the walkway leading to your apartment. Your car is engulfed

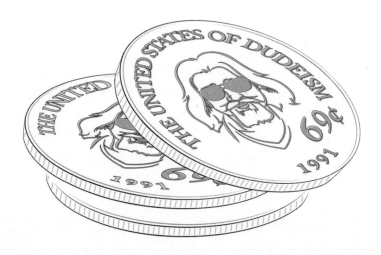

in flames and nihilists are threatening to fuck you ups, but you open your wallet and offer what's in it.

It's the tenth already. You lose a little bit of money.

You can't be worrying about that shit.

When your rug is micturated upon, your response is not to call the cops, despite the fact that your house has been broken into, your doorframe smashed, your porcelain cracked, and your head pushed into your own toilet a few times. You don't think to sue the Big Lebowski for 100 times the cost of the rug. You don't hire a lawyer. You don't send TBL a bill.

You go bowling.

It's only when Walter points out the existence of TBL and that he has the wealth, uh, the resources obviously, and that there is no reason, no *fucking* reason, why his wife should go out and owe money all over town, and they pee on your rug—only then that you get riled up over the injustice of it (not because of the money). You call Brandt, and Brandt fills TBL in. You drive straight to his house, dressed like that on a weekday.

The Big Lebowski has decided, before you both sit down, that you are there to extort money from him. His way of dealing with what he *thinks* you are is to slap you around verbally, so the first words out of his mouth are sarcastic and condescending. Finally, he is shouting.

But you are not shouting. Not about this.

A Dudeist, unlike most of the world, has an innate sense of what's right and wrong, what's worth getting upset over or not. You are there for a rug; it is right that you get the rug, and you take the rug. That you lose it later and receive a sock on the jaw doesn't take away from the fact that you've won a round with a bigger, louder, far more powerful man with two words:

Fuck it.

TBL says you should tattoo it on your forehead, and he's right. It may seem as though he's insulting you when he says, "That's your answer for everything," but he's right.

When Bunny looks you in the eye and says, "I'll suck your cock for a thousand dollars," you don't blink or express disdain or disgust for either the offer or its sky-high price. "Fuck it" translates to "fuck you," which is really what your statement, "Uh, I'm just gonna go find a cash machine," means.

It's only your acute sense of right and wrong that drives you to call the Big Lebowski a "human paraquat" after figuring out he has embezzled money meant to help underprivileged children, and it's your concern for your physical safety that causes you to temporarily lose your center after Uli and the other two nihilists disrupt your bath and threaten castration.

You let the phone ring.

You let the beeper beep.

You know, in your soul, you're not trying to scam anyone here and that so much in life can be dealt with by drinking a White Russian, or inventing your own *tai chi*.

Fuck it.

It's a Dudeist's version of "thy will be done."

EPILOGUE

I Can Get You a Vow

Now that you've reached the end of the trail of this here book we've unfolded, you're ready to go forth and dude-iply.

If you're innerested in joining our community of more than 120,000 ordained Dudeist priests currently abiding around the world, visit dudeism.com/ordination. Ordudenation is free and easy, man, just like our whole laid-back ethos.

As a Dudeist priest, you are called to just take it easy by abiding through all the strikes and gutters that the cosmic bowling alley rolls your way. If you're into the whole taking-priestly-vows thing, these here vows can really help tie your life together as an official member of the Church of the Latter-Day Dude's clergy:

> *As an ordained Dudeist priest, I (state your name) vow:*
> - *To just take it easy, man*
> - *To spread the Dude word when it's not too exhausting*
> - *To always make time to have some burgers, some beers, a few laughs*
> - *To always check in to see what condition my condition is in*
> - *To not treat objects like women, man*
> - *To uh...lost my train of thought there*
> - *To keep my mind limber*

- *To enjoy natural, zesty enterprises while fixing the cable*
- *To never repeat things just because a book instructs me to do so*
- *And always, in a world gone crazy, to abide*

So help me Dude.

Now, Brother Shamuses and Special Ladies, go forth, abide, and to thine own self be Dude.

Lord, you can imagine where it goes from here.

ABOUT THE AUTHORS

Oliver Benjamin founded The Church of the Latter-Day Dude in 2005. His website, dudeism.com, is the hub of hubbub around which the religion of Dudeism rolls. He lives in Thailand and Los Angeles. When not attending to his duties as the Dudely Lama of Dudeism, he does the usual at oliverbenjamin.net.

Dwayne Eutsey serves as the Arch Dudeship of the church and founded its monastic order, The Brotherhood Shamus. He is a writer/editor abiding near a nice, quiet beach community in Maryland with his special lady with whom he helped to conceive their three little Eutsowskis.